Bi-US

The Social Justice of being...

Black in the United States

6th Edition

Featuring:

A seven centuries Chronology with *Commentary*

by *Constance W. Porter*

Historian, and Author

This book is dedicated to my family, and the friends who have each contributed in their own way. My two sons, Dr. Jason W. Porter, was murdered in 2004 (unsolved); and to my second son, Dr. Ian D. Porter, who has blessed me beyond words, and beyond thanks,

TABLE OF CONTENTS

FORWARD 1

TESTIMONIALS... 3

INTRODUCTION... 5

THE AFRICAN EXISTENCE IN NORTH AMERICA 7

The 1400's 9

The 1500's 9

The 1600's 11

INTRODUCTION TO THE 1700'S................................. 17

The 1700's 18

INTRODUCTION TO THE 1800'S................................. 28

The 1800's 30

INTRODUCTION TO THE 1900'S................................. 61

The 1900's 63

INTRODUCTION TO THE 2000'S.............................. 122

2000's.. 123

WHAT NOW BLACK AMERICA?.............................. 133

REFERENCES 135

INDEX 136

FORWARD

I am a Black woman. Born, raised, and educated in the yet-to-be United States of America, I am consistently considered to be at the bottom of the American caste system. This experience is a vestige of slavery; one of many, that this country has not yet come to terms with.

It is easy to blame the education system where we are taught very little about Black people outside of slavery; a curriculum that highlights only part of America's history, by glorifying its greatness and glazing over the parts that continuously impact its minorities. It is because of this spotty education that we have framed a story about ourselves, and this country that is inconsistent with the truth.

This is a time where many Americans of various ethnicities and colors are more open to challenging what has been historically taught about Black Americans. They are seeking and consuming new perspectives, and research on America from Black voices. They are expanding their knowledge base, in an effort to simply understand.

For those looking for resources, allow this book to be one of your guides. Utilizing contemporary research, this wonderful text by Constance W. Porter, details a compelling chronology of the Black experience in America over the course of 7 centuries.

I was awed by her ability to take years of research and distill it into an easy-to-read piece of literature, that also makes sense. As a voracious reader of books on social

1

injustice, this book provided me with a historical chronology that one needs in order to fully understand the Black experience in America.

Karla M. Trotman, MBA

President & CEO, Electro Soft, Inc

TESTIMONIALS

To: Connie Porter

Tuesday, June 18, 2019, 2:44PM

Girl, I want to congratulate you on this book. Larry was also impressed, as I was telling him about, and reading some of it to him. I finished it, and am getting ready to watch one of the movies today that you mentioned.

I wish all black people [especially], had a copy of this book. It is so enlightening and informative. Again, I congratulate you, and am very honored that you allowed me to be among the first to read it. I will be among the first to purchase it.

Portia Frederick

****

Black In the United States is a compilation of laws and experiences of African Americans in the US. The American historical injustices have been going on since time immemorial. This installment gives insight on the evolution of the lifestyle of people of color in the US. This book will give you thrills and keep you at the edge of your seat until the end.

There are a few things to appreciate about this work. Firstly, the sentences are written in point form and different fonts. As a result, it is easy to grasp the notions disseminated in its pages. There is also necessary highlighting and italicization; consequently, it puts more emphasis on a text to show its importance. The volume is full of historical concepts that would be helpful to scholars and lovers of antiquity. Additionally, the grammar employed is straightforward and comprehensible.

I became emotional at some of the points I read from this book. I could not believe people of color were treated quite inhumanely between the 18th and 21st centuries. For instance, in the 18th century, there was "The Negro Slave Act of South Carolina." It was hard to believe the lawmakers could implement an act with such an offensive title.

As I discovered nothing to despise, I rate the book 4 out of 4 stars.

Partial review -Online Book Club

INTRODUCTION

For years I wanted to gain a clearer picture of the African American experience in the United States. In history class, my first question was: how did we go from the Harlem Renaissance to Jim Crow? As I began to research, the WHY's increased. I saw that legislation played a huge part in our freedoms, or restrictions, and our actions.

I noticed that for each century there were cycles of expansion and contraction to black freedoms. I wanted to complete this work because:

1. *How the legal system affected our social life hasn't been explored enough.*
2. *Everyday people should know it, (not just students, or professors).*
3. *Awareness, or knowledge must precede changes in actions and expectations.*
4. *It is relevant to what is happening now.*

I hope that you will gain a new perspective and appreciate the WHAT & WHY about many things.

The descriptive terms of Black, Negro, Colored, African American, Afro-American, and Mulatto (mixed Black & White), are freely exchanged to mean the same thing. It is simply that different terminologies were politically correct at different times. Also know that any numbers listed are simply for a point of reference. They are not exact, because nobody really counted.

Lastly, my goal was to give "OUR History, in OUR Words". That goal made a difference in what has traditionally been told, believed, or omitted by others. This journal limits the usual entertainment, artistic, inventive [etc.] accomplishments of our people, since that would take us in a different direction from the social and justice directive.

Here are three quotes that have fueled my passion:

Henry Louis Gates Jr. posed the question "Where have all our freedoms gone?" in his documentary, "The African Americans, Many Rivers to Cross".

Maulana N Karenga's, 2nd principal of Kwanzaa, "Kujichagulia" meaning "to have Self Determination"; to define ourselves, as well as to create and speak for ourselves. Hence, "Our History, in Our Words".

Jorge Santayana in 1905, and Winston Churchill in 1948: "those who don't know their history are destined to repeat it."

You will notice that with a few exceptions, I have not quoted sources (sometimes it's within the context of the event). I challenge readers to reference at least one entry in this work, to see the rest of the story. Only two pieces of information are needed to cross reference on the internet: 1. A name or title, and 2. a date. In so doing, you will see the challenge of this work; that more than one source is needed to determine what is true, or closest to correct.

And now, for the journey...

THE AFRICAN EXISTENCE IN NORTH AMERICA

What happened worldwide, before Africans arrived in North America, is of great importance. There were wars between countries with naval capabilities. European countries desired to own a piece of the "new world"; to exploit its riches for their own financial stability. Wars between religions would also determine which God would be sovereign; giving them the right, and the need to dominate. Explorers brought the idea "God & Country" with them.

What this history has taught me is...the extent how much African-Americans have contributed to this country; in every phase; in every capacity; from its very beginnings.

Origins

I have gone as far back as I could; to the 1400's; and I have labelled the period between the beginning of slave trade, until the first settlement as PRE-COLONIAL.

Actual trading of African slaves began as early as 1441. The timeline will be more specific.

"The Diaspora" began and continued until England abolished slave trade in 1807 (it didn't end completely). During that time, approximately 12 million Africans were extracted; about 4 million went to South America, about 2

million died en-route; while 4-6 million arrived in the Colonies, and the Caribbean.

King Ferdinand and Queen Isabella of Spain, financed Columbus' expedition (intended for India), along with the Catholic Church. His navigator for the Santa Maria, was a Black Moor, or Afro-Hispanic, named <u>*Pedro Alonzo Nino.*</u> *At the time (1492), there were as many as 10 such navigators; (he was not unusual, according to an article from the Washington Post). Nino also navigated Columbus' third voyage to the Americas.* **Note:** *Christopher Columbus, was half Italian. He lived in; sailed for; and died in* <u>*Spain,*</u> *(the birthplace of his mother, who was from Valencia). All of his voyages went to Central/South America, and the Caribbean Islands.*

It wasn't until after <u>*Florida*</u> *was discovered by Ponce de Leon, in 1513, that North America became involved. Fifty-two years later, in 1565, King Phillip II, of Spain, commissioned* <u>*Commander Francisco Menendez de Aviles*</u> *(who was also a Black Moor), to establish a fort, and neighboring town, to protect Spain's holdings there. The town of* <u>*St. Augustine*</u> *is the first and oldest black town in North America.*

<u>*Fort Mose, and Commander de Aviles,*</u> *were the beginning of an African existence in North America, in 1565. Historically, this is not disputed. Our history has simply been* <u>*Americanized,*</u> *and has never been viewed in context.*

There have always been "free" Africans in North America. We arrived before Jamestown, Virginia, and Plymouth Massachusetts, were established.

The 1400's

Pre-Colonial

1441 It is believed to be the beginning of trading African slaves for goods. It started with a Portuguese explorer, *Antao Concalvez.*

1452 King Charles I, of Spain, (also titled Charles V, Holy Roman Emperor) abolished slavery of American Indians. This did not last. The French did not adhere to this edict.

1455 **Pope Nicolas V, gave a bull *(or edict)* to Portuguese and Spanish traders, to capture and enslave those of African descent who were not *Christian.* This was followed-up by King Charles I, of Spain. The prescribed *permissions and directives* of his edict were *specific, and cruel.*

1492 Pedro Alonzo Nino, a Black Moor, navigated the first, and third (1498) voyages for Christopher Columbus.

The 1500's

1513 Florida, was discovered by Ponce de Leon

1526 Lucas Vasquez Ayllon established San Miguel de Guadalupe (now Georgia). Africans later abandoned this colony. It was the first community using black slaves. They later escaped, and the town was abandoned.

- *Estaban de Dorantes, a Moroccan Black Moor,* explored the territory of what is now Arizona and New Mexico, with *Francisco Vazquez de Coronado.*

1518 King Charles I, of Spain granted the first *license to export African slaves.* They were usually exported to South America, and to the Caribbean.

1562 England officially entered the slave trading enterprise. *Admiral John Hawkins* is acknowledged as the first slave trader for Britain. **Note:** *during the international protest marches for the killing of George Floyd (May 2020), it was Hawkins's statue that was dismantled by the crowd, and thrown into the river, by British protestors.*

1565 Gracia Real de Santa Teresa de Mose [shortened to Fort Mose], was established in Spanish Colonial Florida, to protect Spain's territory from the *French, Dutch, and the British. It was commanded by a Black Moor commissioned officer Francisco Menendez de Aviles.* **Note:** *because this colony was Spanish, it was ignored by American history. The Spanish, including Columbus, were the first to arrive in the Americas.*

San Augustine, Florida; Afro-Hispanic farmers and artisans arrived with Menendez, to establish a settlement approximately 2 miles from Ft. Mose. It was the first community in this new land, and the earliest to be continuously free for African Americans. It still exists today. **Note:** *more recently, Florida has distanced itself from this history. San Augustine is now a resort town,*

1598 Isabel de Olivera, [a mulatto] accompanied explorer *Juan Guerra,* to colonize what is now *New Mexico.*

The 1600's

In this century, many "slave laws" were established by various colonies, to limit activities, and to protect slave ownership. Many of them began in northern colonies. While the English were expanding in the South, the Dutch were expanding the <u>New Netherlands</u>, which included the territories that are now NY, CT, and NJ and MD. New Sweden was mostly the Delaware River banks. Slavery was everywhere.

1603 Mathieu de Costa, explored what is now Canada, and New Amsterdam, now New York.

1607 Jamestown, Virginia was officially founded.

1609 Henry Hudson explored what is now the Hudson River.

Colonial

1613 Juan Rodriquez, a free black sailor, became a trader for the Dutch, on the Native American settlement, in what is now *Manhattan, NY.*

1619 Twenty indentured servants arrived in *Jamestown* on a Dutch ship, <u>before </u>the first British direct slave shipment arrived. ***Note:** indentured means to obtain ship passage in exchange for 4-7 years of unpaid labor, which became common. **Also:** I was first to note this information in 2020, and it changed the internet.*

- *England's* slave ship arrived in *Jamestown, Va.* Formerly, England traded in South America, this was their first *direct shipment to the Colonies.*

1620 The first Pilgrims arrived at Cape Cod, MA. in November. They later formed a settlement in *Plymouth Harbor.* **Note:** *Plymouth was established 13 years after Jamestown; however, St Augustine, FL. (a black colony), was established 55 years before white Europeans arrived.*

1624 Jamestown, became a Royal Colony *(meaning owned by the British).*

1625 African slaves arrived in New Amsterdam, and became the city's first municipal laborers by clearing the lands.

- Dutch West India Company established Ft. Orange (now Albany NY). *1625* Africans slavery began in New Amsterdam.

1629 The first slaves arrived in *Connecticut.*

1636 The Dutch provided for religious schooling of African children (a first), and for Dutch children.

1638 New Sweden (now Delaware) was incorporated into New Netherland.

1640 John Punch, attempted to escape slavery in *Maryland.* He was captured and sentenced to remain *a slave for life.* He was the first legally documented slave.

1641 Massachusetts was the first colony to legalize slavery of *American Indians, along with Whites, and*

Blacks. There, any stranger (and their children), could be legally enslaved.

- *Mathias De Sousa, a* former indentured servant, was elected to *Maryland's General Assembly*.

1642 Maryland introduced slavery.

1645 According to EJI.org, slave trade in the port city of *Boston, MA.,* began around this time, and lasted for two centuries (even beyond banishment laws) While they protested against English rule, they traded goods for slaves between the Caribbean, North America, and England.

- In *New Amsterdam*, slaves who helped in the battles with Native Americans, were granted land. By 1650, they had to relinquish fixed amounts of their crops.

*1649 **Connecticut,* was the first colony to institute a *poll tax (payment to be eligible to vote).* **Note:** *Although we tend to consider poll taxing as a Southern practice; there were 24 states, including northern and western states. It was not until the Civil Rights Era, and the 24th Amendment of 1964, that this practice ended. Voting limitations were replaced by Gerrymandering and Redlining policies.*

1650 Connecticut legalized slavery for hostile Indians and for Africans.

1652 Rhode Island, limited slavery to 10 years of servitude.

- *Massachusetts* legalized military training for Africans. This was later rescinded in 1656.

1653 A wall was built across the Isle of Manhattan to protect the Dutch from the British. It became *Wall Street*.

1655 John Casor, of Virginia, was indentured to A*nthony Johnson (a black slave owner)*. Casor attempted to end his indenture. His owner won a court case, resulting with *him being* designated a *slave for life*. **Note**: *Anthony Johnson, his owner, was of Angolan descent; a former indentured servant; and one of the wealthiest black land owners. Upon his death, Johnson's children could not inherit his estate.*

1662 ****Virginia,** enacted the Hereditary Slavery Law, so *that the child of an enslaved mother* was also a slave. **Note:** *this absolved white fathers of the British law, which allowed children to claim the birthright of the father.*

- *The Royal African Company,* was commissioned in England, for African slave trade.
- Rhode Island abolished slavery, but it did not last. They went or to become a major trans-Atlantic slave trade connection.

1663 South Carolina offered land grants to those who owned 10 or more slaves. This was done to help with the cash crop of rice, and later created a population problem.

- Maryland presumed all blacks to be slaves.

1664 Britain acquired *all the territories* of the New Netherlands. New Amsterdam became New York.

- *The Assembly of Maryland* determined that all blacks and their children would be slaves for life. Also, ownership of weapons or signaling devices were not permitted.

1667 In *England*, an Act declared that Christian baptism of slaves did not exempt them from slavery.

1669 **Virginia,* passed the Casual Killing Act, a law deeming that killing a slave who resisted authority, was not a felony. *Note: does this ring any bells for you concerning police killings?*

1670 **Massachusetts, approved the s*eparation, and sale* of children of enslaved parents.

1673 ** Massachusetts* enacted that *Europeans cannot conduct commerce with African Americans.*

1676 Bacon's Rebellion, was an attempt to create an armed war with the *American Indians.* The goal was to retrieve lands granted to them, by treaty with the VA.(Britis*h) Governor;* thereby allowing homesteaders to own the lands. *Native Americans and Blacks* fought in this rebellio*n. Note: The Plains Wars (1850-70) did exactly that, as settlers established territorial rights of the Louisiana Purchase. Also: do not miss the indication that blacks fought to keep their lands as well.*

1682 **Virginia enacted Slave Codes,* concerning travel; and gun ownership; along with a 4-hour limit on the presence of black non-slaves. *Note: although many historians indicate that 1705, was the beginning of slave codes, this entry contradicts that.*

- *The French settled in Louisianna.*

1690 Carolina passed laws that restricted slave movement.

1691 **Virginia,** voted to ban *miscegenation (inter-racial marriage) White men were not allowed to marry;* a white woman paid a fine, and 5 years servitude if they birthed mulatto children. Such children became property of the church for 30 years. *[referenced by Gilder Lehrman Institute].* **Note:** *At a time when servitude was a mixture of indentured servants and slaves, anti-miscegenation became an issue. Laws against it were designed to divide and conquer, and to prevent mixed co-operation between black and white due to social proximity.*

- *The Province of Carolina was split into North and South Carolina. North Carolina did not support plantations.*

1696 Quakers threatened expulsion from the church for those who owned slaves.

** *Laws that affected Black futures*

The Colonial laws that were established in the 1600's, carried forth for centuries.

INTRODUCTION TO THE 1700'S

In the previous century, when Colonies were just becoming established, we saw the inclusion of slavery, and colonial laws to maintain control. Slavery was not just a Southern phenomenon, it was everywhere.

By far, the most meaningful event of the century was the Declaration of Independence, and the Revolutionary War (from 1775 to 1783). The common goal was self-rule, instead of foreign territorial ownership. The establishment of the United States of America was anything but United; but they did band together on that accord.

In the 1700's a colony's designation became a dividing factor for slave or free territories. By the end of the century, six of the Northern colonies were declared as "free" colonies or states.

Those colonies dependent on the economics of slave labor feared the loss of an economic commodity, as well as power, privilege, and rebellions. Their diverse approaches created a division that has never healed. While Northern colonies/states allowed for the education and contributions of the African population, they found other ways to limit black inclusion, in the affairs of the new nation. Population imbalance created great fear.

The 1700's

1700 The port city *of Boston* was the largest settlement in the Americas.

1702 **New York* passed a law prohibiting slaves from testify in court against whites.

1704 Elias Neau, established the *School for People of* Color (free or slave). in New York.

1705 **In Virginia,* all <u>non-Christian</u> servants were determined to be slaves. Interracial marriage was also forbidden.

1708 Africans outnumbered whites in the state of *South Carolina; a threat to white rule, with future consequences.*

1711 Queen Ann of Great Britain, overturned a *Pennsylvania law, which had prohibited slavery.*

- *A slave market* was established at the end of *Wall Street, in New York City.*
- ***New York,* passed a law outlawing land inheritance, for free and enslaved blacks.

1712 The New York Slave Revolt occurred on April 6th, with 23 blacks and 9 whites killed, resulting in new slave codes.

1713 England, secured an exclusive right from the Spanish to transport slaves to the Colonies.

- *Rhode Island began* trading Rum to England in exchange for slaves to the sugar plantations in the

Caribbean; thus, becoming a major port destination in the slave transport triangle.

1717 Louisiana, established slavery.

1718 The city of *New Orleans* was officially founded by the French. At the time, there were more enslaved blacks than whites.

1721 ***South Carolina,* limited voting, to *only free white Christian men; only those owning 10 slaves could vote.*

1724 Code Noir, (black codes), were established in *Louisiana.*

- The city of *Boston, Ma.* established a curfew for non-whites.

1729 The Natchez Revolt, made by the Natchez Native Americans of Mississippi and enslaved blacks, against the cruelty of their French masters. The result was the decimation of the Natchez Tribe.

1735 South Carolina, legislated that slave clothing must be identifiable, and of low-quality fabric.

1739 The Stono Rebellion or Cato's Rebellion occurred in South Carolina. A band of approximately 20-50 slaves marched 15 miles toward Ft. Mose Florida, while burning 6 plantations and killing 20-25 whites on the way.

1740 The Negro Act of 1740. South Carolina passed laws which permitted rebellious slaves to be , by death (not considered a crime).

1741 The New York Conspiracy Trails, also called the *Negro Plot,* established a "witch hunt", concerning 13 suspicious fires in the state of New York

- *South Carolina* banned the **teaching** of reading and writing **to blacks.** They also limited assembly, of black, and the possibility of earning money.

1746 Lucy Terry wrote a poem, *The First Bar Fight,* concerning an Indian raid in Massachusetts.

1750 Antoine Benezet, an abolitionist Quaker of Philadelphia undertook to educate black children and their schooling at his home. By 1754, he created a secondary school for girls, and convinced Quakers to build a school for blacks by 1770.

1753 Benjamin Banneker, a black mathematician and clock maker, was commissioned; along with 5 others, to design the layout of Washington, DC.

1758 Dr. Thomas *Bray & Associates* established a free school in Philadelphia, Pa.

- *Bluestone Church* of Mecklenburg, Va. was established.

1760 A narrative,*" the uncommon sufferings and surprising deliveries, of Briton Hammon, a negro man",* was written.

1761 Jupiter Hammon, was the first African *poet* and slave to be published, in New York.

1762 *Virginia* established that only white males could vote.

1768 *General George Washington* purchased William and his brother Frank. *Wm. (Billy) Lee* became his trusted companion during the war. He is depicted in several paintings of Washington, and was later freed.

1770 General Washington allowed free black men to enlist in the Continental Army.

- *Crispus Attucks*, was among those killed, while taunting British soldiers, on March 5th. in what became known *as The Boston Massacre.* This event was said to be among pre-cursors to the War of Independence/Revolutionary War.

1773 *Phyllis Wheatley,* became the first *female* African American to *be published.*

1774 *First African Baptist, church of Savannah, GA.* was established, and was co-pastored by Andrew Bryan (who was one of three co-founding ministers of the *Silver Bluff* congregation.

- *The Society for the Relief of Free Negros Unlawfully Held in Bondage*, was established, and later became known as the *Pennsylvania Abolition Society.*
- *Lord Dunmore, the British Governor of the Virginia Colony,* issued a Proclamation to recruit enslaved Africans. They offered freedom and paid service, in exchange for loyalty to the British. ***Note:*** *after the end of the War of Independence, former black*

soldiers were sent to Sierra Leone, Liberia, London,
Spanish Colonial Florida, and Jamaica. As a
result, more blacks served for the British than the
Continentals.

- *General George Washington, discontinued* enlistment of blacks in the Continental Army. *In 1776 he reverses that decision.*

THE REVOLUTIONARY WAR, *or* **War of Independence** *began, in 1775 and lasted until 1783. Approximate 20,000 blacks served for the British, and 5,000 for the Continentals. Throughout the war, approximately 100,000 slaves fled their masters.*

 THE DECLARATION OF INDEPENDENCE, was drafted on July 4th, 1776, *by Thomas Jefferson, and signed on August 2nd.* **Note:** *Hereafter,* **Colonies** *became known as* **States**. *The issue of slavery was omitted from the Declaration, due to pressure from the slave states.*

THE PRE-COLONIAL PERIOD ENDED

1777 Vermont, became the first colony to *ban slavery (they gained statehood on July 2, 1791).*

1778 The 1st Rhode Island Regiment; a black fighting unit, (which was 62% black, and included Indigenous men), was established, and served for the Continentals. They were most known for *the Battle of Yorktown (in 1781);* they served the entire war. **Note:** *The Black Brigade, and the Ethiopian Regiment served for the British, during the war.*

1780 Pennsylvania, adopted the *Act of Gradual Abolition of Slavery.* It provided that *children of slaves were free,* and stopped the importation of slaves. It also repeals anti-miscegenation laws.

- *Paul Cuffe, of Massachusetts, was a black shipping magnate and activist;* who eventually became one of the richest blacks in the US. He refused to pay taxes (along with 5 others) on the grounds that free blacks could not vote, and were not represented in the system.
- *John Hanson, a black merchant from Maryland,* became the first *President of the Continental Congress,* while the nation was forming. He served from 1780-1782; longer than the following 13 (until George Washington was elected as President of the USA in 1789).
- *John Baptist Point De Sable,* founded a *trading post* for west-bound settlers that eventually became *the city of Chicago (by 1837).*
- *Slavery was abolished in Massachusetts,* and they were given the right to vote. *1783 A*pproximately 3,000 *black loyalist troops* were relocated to *Nova Scotia, with land grants (as promised by the British).*

1780 The Act for Gradual Abolition of Slavery was enacted in *Pennsylvania (*females at 18, males at 21, and newborns free).

1784 Connecticut, and Rhode Island, adopted gradual emancipatio*n.*

- *The New York African Free Society* was started as a benevolent association to free blacks.

1785 New York allowed slaves who served in the War to be freed.

1787 Prince Hall, established the first African *Masonic Lodge # 439, in* Philadelphia, PA. It was chartered by the *Grand Masonic Lodge of England.*

- *Prince Hall & Absalom Jones* established the African Free Society in Phila. Pa.
- *New York* freed all slaves who served in the Revolutionary Army.
- *The New York Free School* was established to educate the newly freed.
- *The New York African Free Society was* established for benevolence.
- *The Congress of the Confederation of US* enacted the **Northwest Ordinance.** It gave procedures to admit territories into the *Union;* addressed religious freedom; and other rights. **Note:** *Moving forward, you will see how this ordinance was changed, and the bitter fights over the designation of free or slave state.*
- *At the Constitutional Convention,* **The 3/5 Compromise,** insured that *slave states* could gain additional representation by apportioning 3/5 of the slave population to represent one, in congress. **Note:** *this was written into the Constitution, and would not be repealed until the 14th Amendment of 1868. It is where the division of our country began There were several compromises, so that the*

Constitution could be ratified. The Electoral College, and the Great Compromise for two legislative houses were also written in.

1788 the United States Constitution was ratified.

THE UNITED STATES OF AMERICA was established in 1989. *George Washington was inaugurated as the first President, as elected by vote, and by the Electoral College.*

The COLONIAL ERA ended

1790 The Brown Fellowship was established in Charlston, SC., as an elite benevolent fellowship for mulattos. Later it became *the Century Followship.*
- *Toussaint L'Ouverture,* a Frenchman, successfully led revolts in Haiti. Eventually, he was betrayed and hung in 1802. His efforts helped to hasten the end of slave trade.

The United States Constitution was ratified on **Dec 15th**. *Amendments 1 through 10 were included:*

The AMENDMENTS

1 gave the right to peaceful assembly, freedom of speech, religion, and the press

2 gave the right to a well-regulated militia and the right to bear arms

3 gave the right to refuse to quarter soldiers in home without permission, in peace or war as allowed

4   provides security against unreasonable search and seizure without warrant or probable cause

5   declared no person can be held to witness against themselves and no double jeopardy in trials

6   gave the right to a public and speedy trial and the assistance of counsel.

7   gave the right to be tried by a jury.

8   provided protection against cruel and unusual punishment for those imprisoned and against untenable fines and bail.

9   gave *Unremunerated (or to be determined later)* rights regarding travel, voting, privacy, and health decisions.

10   clarified, that any rights of the Federal Government not listed, belong to the States unless changed by the Constitution.

1791 Benjamin Banneker was among the surveyors of Washinton, DC. He published an *Almanac* in 1792.

*1793 **The Fugitive Slave Act**,* was passed (the first of 2), whereby Congress made it illegal to harbor escaped slaves; and *allowed that escaped slaves must be returned to their former owners. **Note** it is generally claimed that the Underground Railroad was put in place by abolutuionists from 1800-1865. However, this new Act was intended to deter abolitionist efforts*

   • *Eli Whitney,* applied for a patent of the Cotton Gin (which extracts seed from cotton). This made cotton a *"cash crop"* and doubled the slave states from 7 to 15; while exponentially increasing slave trade.

1794 Rev. Richard Allen, established the Mother
Bethel African Methodist Episcopal (AME) Church in
Philadelphia. Pa. Two years later, he organized AME's
nationally. He became their first bishop. ***Note:*** *his first
church was established at a blacksmith shop. He was
born a slave in Delaware, but purchased his freedom at
age 18, and became a minister by 1984. He established
schools for freedmen, and was part of the Underground
Railroad.*

- *Absalom Jones* established the African Episcopal
  Church *of St. Thomas, in Philadelphia.*

1797 Absalom Jones became the first Worshipful Master
of a Masonic Lodge.

1798 Joshua Johnston of Baltimore, was an artist and
the first to publish *an ad* concerning his works.

1799 New York granted freedom to all slaves.

INTRODUCTION TO THE 1800'S

In the early 1800's, our new government, (which was only 11 years old), began the process of becoming a nation. Laws and policies were determined, hopefully within the new Constitution. Aside from the differences between the North and South, the West came into the picture. The economics of slavery had to be dealt with, especially whether a state would be <u>slave or free</u>; as well as State Laws versus Federal laws; and balancing Congressional representation.

The 1800's had a huge impact on the future of the USA. It is where the attitudes towards the African American population were <u>entrenched</u>, for centuries to come.

The War of 1812, and the Civil War were the most outstanding events. Our timeline shows the various events that led up to them, politically and socially.

The Reconstruction Era, and the involvement of Blacks in the political arena lit a match that exploded into big drama and violence. Voting became the new "battlefront" after the Civil War. The lines between supremacist right, and liberal left were drawn. They remain in place today.

The Era was jammed with drama; the Wars the Underground Railroad; the Dred v. Scott decision; Secession from the Union, Civil War; Reconstruction; Juneteenth; the KKK, & Redshirts; Black Laws; the 14th & 15th Amendments; sharecropping, massacres, segregation; Financial Panics, the Cholera Epidemic (of the 1870's), the

Presidential Election of 1876; and the North Carolina Coup d'etat of 1899; are all on the list.

Actress Betty Davis was right in saying "<u>Fasten your seat belts, it's gonna be a bumpy ride</u>" (in the movie All About Eve, 1950).

All the drama, legislation, heroes, villains, plots and plans, and court rulings, are waiting to be re-discovered.

The 1800's

1800 Gabriel Prosser, of Virginia, was an educated blacksmith, who was routinely hired-out for work on other plantations. He planned Gabriel's Rebellion, which involved several counties. His plans were betrayed, and he was eventually hung; along with his two brothers, and 23 others. ***Note:*** *this revolt created fear of the outnumbering black population, and resulted in African travel limitations for slaves and freemen, in Virginia, and other the states, by 1803.*

1803 The Louisiana Purchase was made between *the US and France,* who gave up rights to colonize this territory. Included were the states of. CO, IO, KS, OK, ND, NE, SD, MN, MT, NM, & WY, along with LA, AR, and MO, and TX. It doubled the size of the United States, with six free states among them. ***Note:*** *originally, France gained this territory from a treaty with Bonapart and Spain.* It doubled the size of the United States, with six free states among them. Settling this territory *caused the* <u>*Plains War*</u> *between the US and Indigenous "Indians" in the mid 1850's.*

1804 Ohio, became the first *free state* to enforce Black Codes/Laws, which limited movement by blacks.

- *An African American,* accompanied Lewis *& Clark's* expeditions of Louisiana, and the Midwest. He was only known as *York.* He was a frontiersman, and a bondsman to *Lewis.*
- ***The 12th Amendment to the Constitution*** *was approved.* It established the <u>*Electoral College,*</u> *to*

assure that a President <u>cannot be</u> elected solely by the popular vote (designed to limit the possibility of a dictatorship via controlled elections).

1807 New Jersey passed a law stating only white men could vote.

- *Congress banned, and England abolished,* importing slaves in ships (often ignored).
- *Delaware passed an* anti-miscegenation law.
- ***Pace v. Alabama,*** *the United States Supreme* Court upheld Alabama's law against interracial marriage (anti-miscegenation).

1808 The Third Battalion of Royal and Colonial Marines, was established as a salaried, black *British* army. They were active until 1815, and they served in the northeast, until disbanded and freed.

1809 Marriage within the African American community was recognized by the state of New York.

1810 The African Insurance Company of the USA (Phila., PA.) was the first to be black owned.

1811 Andry's Rebellion, was led by *Charles Deslondes,* on the Louisiana plantation *of Manuel Andry. It* was a two-day event; that involved up to 500 slaves, of several plantations, and was quelled by state militia.

THE WAR OF 1812 *started when the British began an economic blockade that involved taxing and attacking US shipping; thus, preventing international trade, (cotton). The USA allied with France, against the British. Native*

*Americans were aligned with the British.to save their tribal lands from settlers. The war lasted two years and 8 months, until 1815. It was fought in the US, and Canada. Most noted events were the **burning of the Capitol building in Washington, DC**, by the British, (which inspired the Star-Spangled Banner); the Battle of New Orleans; and Fort McHenry. <u>African American war heroes were</u>: General Joseph Savary, George Roberts, Charles Ball, Jordan Noble, and William Williams. It ended with the Treaty of Ghent, whereby, Britian released any claim to the Midwest; and ended British and French slave trade. Although it promoted pride in the US, it left many territorial disputes un-resolved. This war finished what the War of Independence started.*

- *Boston* allowed black free schools to become part of their education system.

1816 Rev. Dr. Charles Finley, an abolitionist, established *The American Colonization Society.* His efforts helped to relocate Africans to what became *Liberia,* a free African country, (by 1822). The society raised funds to transport up to 15,000 Freedmen, and 3,000 Afro-Caribbeans.

1817 Escaped slaves from GA, SC, and AL joined with the Seminole tribes of Florida, to keep their homelands.

*1818 **Connecticut's Constitution*** limited voting rights to whites only.

*1820 **The Missouri Compromise,*** allowed that 2 states could be admitted to the Union at a time (one slave, and one free state). The idea was to keep a balanced representation in the Senate. In Missouri, there was great contention over the Presidential Election, as to whether it was a slave or free state.

- *Thomas Jennings* invented the dry-cleaning process.
- *New York* required property ownership, in order for black males to vote.

1822 Denmark Vassey, a freedman, plotted a rebellion to take over Charleston, SC. It never happened. Vassey, and 34-37 others were betrayed and hanged.

1826 Levi Coffin, a white Quaker abolitionist, moved from South Carolina to the free state of *Indiana.* Here, his home became known as the *Grand Central Station of the Underground Railroad* (due to its central location). He and his wife assisted more than 3,000 to freedom and taught trades to some. He later moved to Cincinnati. He had a 20- year legacy of assisting slaves (see the movie *Emperor,* 2020).

1827 Freedom's Journal, the first black owned weekly news publication, began.

- *Theodore Sedgewick,* was the first black graduate of *Princeton Theological Seminary.*
- *The term Jim Crow* became popular at this time. It is the shortened version of *Jump Jim Crow; a Minstrel Show* song and dance by *Thomas Dartmouth.* He performed it in blackface; to the entertainment of whites. The term stuck. The N---- word was used, and the negative characterizations stuck too. *It also contained political commentary. A verse from Dartmouth's song:*

"Should dey get to fighting,

Perhaps de blacks will rise,

For deir wish for freedom,

Is shining in deir eyes"; quoted from Wikipedia

1828 New York became a free state when its decree for gradual emancipation was matured.

1829 The Cincinnati Race Riots occurred from the 15th to 22nd of August. An increasing black presence was competition to unfriendly white skilled laborers. Whites *attacked and routed 1, to 1.5 thousand* blacks to leave the state. At the time, Ohio already had black laws in place (which began in 1807).

- *David Walker,* a black abolitionist, published *"To Black Citizens of the World"*. It urged slaves to rebel; masters to emancipate; abolitionists to help; and for changes in legislature.

1830 **The Indian Removal Act of 1830,** signed by *Pres. Jackson,* set the stage for the new country's approach to the indigenous population. When attempted treaties could not be maintained, war and near annihilation became reality for the next three generations.

1831 The Nat Turner Rebellion occurred in *Virginia.* It caused the death of at least 51 whites, and promoted fear among white owners. Reprisals killed at least 200. Turner was caught and hanged.

1831 Historically this year is quoted as the beginning of *The Underground Railroad.* **Note:** *For consideration, we have seen that escape routes, and destinations to Ft Mose, were in place in the 1700's. You could say, this is when it was recognized. The URR helped more than 75,000 freedom seekers over the next 30 years, until the beginning of the Civil War, in 1861.*

1832 The Georgia Infirmary was considered the first hospital for African Americans. Chartered in December, it gave care to slaves who were old, or ill.

1833 The Boston Female Anti-Slavery Society was founded in *Massachusetts, and in Philadelphia, PA.* Both organizations were interracial abolitionist groups, that lobbied for legislative change, and supported *Underground Railroad* activities

1834 Henry Blair, received a patent for a corn planting machine. **Note:** *this entry was a long-standing source of historical mis-information.*

- *African Free Schools* became part of the *New York Public School system.*
- *South Carolina,* banned education for Africans, *whether free or enslaved.*
- *David Ruggles,* an abolitionist, opened the first black owned African American *book store in New York, at the age of 24.* His reading room spread information for abolitionist support; he also helped to establish the Underground Railroad.

1836 The Battle of San Jacinto, and "Remember the Alamo", gave Texas independence from Mexico. Texas remained a slave territory, which was a factor in their fight against Mexico.

- *The House of Representatives passed the Gag Rule: to prevent discussion, or legislation regarding slavery (1836-1844).*

1837 The Institute for Colored Youth, was founded in Pennsylvania. It later became *Cheyney State University.*

1837 The Philadelphia Vigilance Committee/Association, was organized to help support and finance the Underground Railroad, and escaped slaves.

1838 Pennsylvania, adopted *voting privileges for white males only.*

1839 The Spanish ship La Amistad, had fifty-three slaves enroute to *Cuban* servitude. They mutinied, and sailed to *New York. They were moved to Connecticut, a free state.* Two years later, *in 1841, a Supreme Court* ruled on their behalf, and granted the remaining slaves fr*eedom. This was possibly through abolitionist efforts. (see the movie* Amistad, 1997)

1841 Frederick Douglass, along with white abolitionist *William Lloyd Garrison,* collaborated to publish *Dismantling Slavery.* Their friendship created important public discourse in the North, and in Europe.

1842 The Dorr Rebellion was about an elite group of governing officials led by Thomas Dorr, of Rhode Island, when citizens rebelled against Dorr's restrictive proposals. A revised state constitution resulted, which broadened voting rights in 1843. Note: *Frederick Douglass was involved in this change.*

- ***Prigg v. Pennsylvania,*** the USSC ruled that extraditing former slaves to their *ownership-state* was not required, thereby reversing the *Fugitive Slave Act of 1793.*

1843 Rev. Henry Highland Garnet, gave an Address to Slaves. A notable quote: "Neither God, nor angels, or just men, command you to suffer for a single moment".

The Mexican American War began in April, 1844. *It concerned the annexation of Texas, and territorial borders. It lasted two years. Buffalo Soldiers fought in this war.*

- ***The Territory of Oregon,*** *passed a law* that their *population remain white only.*
- *William Still,* began service of 21 years i*n the Underground Railroad, in Philadelphia.* He became known as the *Father of the Underground Railroad,* assisting more than 800, to freedom.
- **North Carolina legislated that *African Americans were NOT CITIZENS* of the United States. (see the Dred Scott decision of 1857)

1845 Macon Bolling Allen, became the first black to be admitted-to-the-*Bar Association,* to practice law in *Massachusetts.*

1846 Missouri, passed laws to allow interstate slave trade.

1847 Missouri, prohibited education of *Freedmen.*

- *David J. Peck,* became the first African American *(in this country),* to become a doctor; by graduating Rush Medical School, in Chicago, IL.

Note: *the two entries for 1847 are in direct opposition.*

1848 Women's Suffrage, experienced a boost when Frederick Douglass (and other men) supported them, by attending *the Women's Right Convention, in Seneca Falls, NY.*

The California Gold Rush began.

1849 **The Treaty of Guadalupe Hidalgo,** ended the *War with Mexico, (which began in 1846). T*he USA gained the territories of *Texas, California, New Mexico, Nevada, Utah, Wyoming, Arizona, Colorado and parts of Wyoming, Oklahoma, and Kansas.* This expanded the US from coast to coast; the Rio Grande River was determined as the *southern border of the US.*

- *Harriette Tubman,* escaped from slavery. She later returned to the south, to be part of the *Underground Railroad,* and became known as the *Conductress of the Underground Railroad.* Her legacy was to aid more than 300 slaves to freedom.

The Plains Wars began around this time. *There were infamous battles between the US Government and the indigenous tribes of the Northern Plains (between the Mississippi River and the Rocky Mountains). Buffalo Soldiers participated in these wars also. There were massacres, and mass cruelty on both sides, as the "Indians" fought to keep their homelands; while* *homesteaders fought to populate the Louisiana Purchase. Cowboys & Indians were very real.*

1851 **The Compromise of 1850,** admitted *California as a free state;* established a boundary for *Texas; and* abolished slavery in *Washington, DC.* **Note:** *As new territories became states, determining whether they would be slave or free states, created huge conflicts.*

- **The Fugitive Slave Act of 1850,** was enacted to *re-enforce the Act of 1793; and* was also in opposition to the Supreme *Court's* **Prigg v. Pennsylvania ruling, of 1842.** However, the return of escaped slaves became *a Federal* responsibility with this *Act.* This created *federal slave catchers;* it was opposed to in northern states.
- *The American League of Colored Workers,* was established as the first black trade union, in NY.

1851 Sojourner Truth, was the name chosen by *Isabell Baumfree,* a former slave and abolitionist. She was most noted for her speech, *"Ain't I a Woman?",* given at the Ohio Women's Rights Convention.

1852 Hariett Beecher Stowe; an abolitionist, published *Uncle Tom's Cabin. It* was a bestseller, and helped to turn opinions against the *Fugitive Slave Act.*

1853 William Wells Brown, was credited for being the first published black *novelist.* His book was *"Clotel, the President's Daughter".* As an orator, he was a gifted speaker, both *here and in England (where he also lived).* Brown was an abolitionist; active in the Underground

Railroad; and shared concerns with Frederick Douglass, and William Lloyd Garrison.

1854 Anthony Burns, was kidnapped as a slave escapee. His recapture in *Boston,* caused protests, and martial law; as *federal catchers* extradited him back to Virginia, under the *Fugitive Slave Act of 1850.*

- **The Kansas-Nebraska Act,** *was p*assed by Congress, to repeal the *Missouri Compromise,* and to allow Kansas and Nebraska into the Union as *slave states.*
- *"Bleeding Kansas" was* the term used concerning 4 years of armed battles between pro and anti-slavery factions, regarding Kansas' free or slave state *designation.* **Note:** *Kansas eventually entered the Union as a free state in 1861.These events were also precursors to the Civil War.*
- *The Republican Party* was established in Michigan, to oppose admitting slavery into western territories. **Note:** *in its beginning, the Republican Party was liberal, and anti-slavery.*
- *James A. Healy,* became the first black ordained Jesuit priest. Eighteen years later, he became Bishop of a diocese that included Maine, and New Hampshire.

1855 Massachusetts, outlawed racially segregated schools.

- *William C. Nell,* published the first black history book–*The Colored Patriots of the American Revolution.*

- *John Mercer Langston,* became the first black elected official, in the state of *Ohio.*
- *Frederick Douglas,* published *My Bondage, My Freedom.*

1856 Wilberforce University, was established by the *African Methodist Episcopal Church*, as the first black owned and operated educational institution.

1857 **The Dred Scott Decision of the US Supreme Court,** *or* **Scott v. Sanford,** *was a landmark* USSC decision, which ruled that the US Constitution *did NOT include blacks* because they were *NOT considered citizens of the United States.*

1858 Arkansas began to *conscript Freedmen* into slavery; if they refused to leave the state.

1859 Harriette Wilson, was the first black female to publish a *novel.*

- *John Brown's Raid on Harper Ferry {WV},* was led by Brown and Gerrit Smith, at the Federal Arsenal. The two white abolitionists, along with 16 men (that included 5 blacks), desired to create an emancipated army and a free state. They were never joined by others, and surrendered 2 days later.

South Carolina, seceded from the Union, on Dec 20, 1860. **Note:** *this was another precursor to the Civil War.*

1861 **The First Confiscation Act,** denied slave-owners the ability to re-enslave runaways. **Note;** *Until this Act,* *slave catching was done on the federal level. (see the movie, 12 Years A Slave, 2013).*

- ***The Ordinance of Secession*** *was drafted by Jefferson Davis. It created the* **Confederacy,** *in order to be removed from the Union: AL, SC, GA, FL, LA, and MS were the first; later joined by TX, VA, AR, NC, and TN.*

THE CIVIL WAR began, and lasted 4 years, until 1865.

- *The First Louisiana Native Guard* was organized as the only black unit to fight for the South. ***Note:*** *The 54th & 55th Massachusetts Infantry, the 5th Cavalry; the 1st Carolina Volunteers; the 24th & 25th Texas Cavalry, the 31st Regiment, and the 29th & 30th Connecticut Infantry served for the North.*
- *Robert Smalls,* was conscripted by the *Confederacy.* As the captain of a munitions ship, he commandeered it, and turned it over to the Union. By 1868, Smalls was a *Congressman for SC.*

1863 ***The Emancipation Proclamation,*** took effect on Jan. 1st, legally freeing all slaves; over the opposition of southern states.

- *The New York Draft Riots* resulted when the Union attempted to establish armed service drafts. The eligible men of NY were determined not to serve. The riots lasted 4 days, with a death toll of approximately 100. (see the movie, Street Gangs of NY, 2002).

- *Fort Wagner, of Charleston, SC,* was strategically located, as a Confederate fort. It was finally overtaken, after many attempts, by a *black fighting unit* for the Union, the *54th Volunteer Infantry (see the movie "Glory"-1989)*
- *The Combahee River Raid, of SC,* occurred when 150 black soldiers freed 750 plantation slaves. Col. James Montgomery (Union), enlisted the help of *Harriett Tubman,* to help replenish black regiments.

1864 The Fort Pillow Massacre in TN, occurred as a retaliation by Confederates, for their loss at *Fort Wagner.* It is listed as *a massacre,* because approximately 600 inhabitants surrendered, but approximately 300 blacks were murdered, instead of being taken as prisoners of war.

- *June Crumpler,* was the first black woman to earn a medical degree, at Boston's New England Female Medical College.
- **The Equal Pay Act of 1864,** provided parity for black soldiers, concerning pay, equipment, arms, and health care.

1865 The 13th Amendment was added to the Constitution, abolishing involuntary servitude, *except as a criminal punishment. In order to retrieve their former slave workforce, local laws were passed to criminalize former slaves for what would be minor offenses, (like loitering). They were known as Pig Laws (i.e. accusations of theft etc.).*

- *On January 16th Gen. Sherman issued <u>Field Order #15</u>, to give abandoned lands in SC, FL, and GA, to former slaves found homeless. **Note:** the "<u>Forty Acres and A Mule</u>" did not happen. Sherman's decree was rescinded by President Andrew Johnson, in the fall. **Also:** The lands gained from Confederates, were returned to their original owners. (see the movie Gone With the Wind). **Also:** a <u>mule</u> was not part of the field order.*
- *The Freedmen's Bureau was established by the federal government, for the relief and aid of the newly freed.*

The Civil War ended *when Confederate General Robert E Lee, surrendered to Union General Ulysses S Grant, on <u>April 9th</u>. The heart of Confederacy never ended.*

- *Juneteenth was celebrated as Major General Gordon Granger of the US Army, gave the news that 250,00 slaves in Texas, were now free. They were the last to know.*
- *<u>The Ku-Klux-Klan,</u> or KKK, was founded on December 24th, in Pulaski, TN, by a group of former Confederate Army Veterans, associated with the Knights of the Golden Circle. **Note:** they were an extremist right-wing group, who reigned terror against blacks, in reaction to the 13th Amendment.*

*1866 **The Civil Rights Act of 1866,** declared that <u>all persons born in the United States</u> <u>are now citizens,</u> without regard to race, color, or previous condition. **Note:** this was a reversal of the Dred-Scott Decision of 1857. It is also a prime example of how laws are set aside over time,* *or ignored when unpopular.* **Also***: a current example is the rescinding or reversals being experienced by the Hispanic population's regarding rights to citizenship.*

- ***The Army Organization Act*** *was* enacted by Congress, which created 6, all black army regiments. The 9th and 10th Cavalry, and the 24th and 25th Infantry & Regiments, for black soldiers. They fou*ght* in the *Spanish American, Philippian, and Plains Wars,* to become known as *the Buffalo Soldiers.*

Jim Crow started around this time, *11 years after the war. It was the social response, added to the legal responses of Pig Laws; Black Codes; and Black Laws.* This social shift*, when added to law, managed the post-Civil War experience against blacks. Resentment; fear of job competition; fear of armed Africans; plantation crop losses; population imbalance; and the possibility of voting/political power; or their financial insolvency, were in the mix.*

- *Fisk University,* an HBCU, was founded in January, with funds provided by the Freedmen's Bureau, in TN.

1867 **The Reconstruction Act of 1867,** gave conditions whereby a State that had seceded from the Union, could be re-admitted. It also put *limitations on former Confederates,* they were not allowed to vote, or hold public, or any governing offices.

> **The "RECONSTRUCTION ERA", followed the Reconstruction Act of 1867**

By 1865, the end of the Civil War; the 13th Amendment; and the assassination of Pres. Lincoln brought about a significant shift in the treatment and the approach to managing the black population. Freedom from slavery, did not mean equality, or parity, or social acceptance. Social in-justice was the continued means of controlling the Blacks; legally; psychologically; socially; and financially. Slave States never gave up their concept of ownership and control (even to this day). The <u>Civil War</u> simply changed to <u>"The Social-Political War"</u>. The ingrained resistance to black progress, became <u>national,</u> and <u>political</u> in scope.

- *The Memphis Massacre occurred on May 1st-3rd* concerned a political meeting that was raided by the (mostly Irish) police force, who were in league with the Democratic mayor. **Note:** *reminder, former Confederates could not hold public office.*
- *The New Orleans Massacre,* occurred on July 30th It concerned a demonstration by black freedmen, who were attacked by white rioters.
- *The Knights of the White Camellia,* were established as an upper-class, Democratic, political, white terrorist group, in Louisiana; in opposition to the Civil Rights *Act* of 1866, and the Reconstruction Act of 1867. **Note**: *the organization lasted until 1870.*
- **The Territorial Suffrage Act,** gave African Americans the right to vote in western territories, on January 10th.
- *Morehouse College (an HBCU) was* founded in Atlanta, GA as Augusta Institute.

- *Howard University,* was founded on March, 2nd, in Washington, DC.

1868 **The Fourteenth Amendment** was added, giving those born in the United States *birthright to citizenship;* promised *equal protection under law*; and allowed men aged 21, one *full vote.*

- *The Opelousas Massacre* occurred on September 28th, in *Louisiana, to deter* African American *voting.* A black educator/news publisher was killed for his ideals, along with 150-300, others by the KKK, and Knights of the White Camellia. (resembling the *Black Wall Street Massacre).*

John Willis Menard, a French Creole, was elected to Congress in Louisiana, but was never admitted to serve his term.

1869 John Lewis Ruffin, was the first black to attain a law degree from *Harvard Law School.*

1870 **The 15th Amendment** was added, to *prohibit* both State or Federal *denial* to vote, for all citizens.

- *Thomas Mundy Peterson,* became the first African American to vote, in Perth Amboy, NJ

The Cholera epidemic from abroad reached the United States.

- **The Enforcement Act of 1870-1971,** prohibited black voter discrimination by state, and specified penalties *with government intervention*; it also provided *equal protection under the law*.

Sharecropping became more widespread around this time. *Although sharecroppers are usually depicted as black, they actually represented only 1/3. (see the movie Sounder); **Also:** the play, Perlie Victorious, which illustrated real economic conditions, i.e.* sharecropping and the company store. It was slavery revised.

- *The KKK* began including voter fraud, and voter intimidation into their tactics.

1871 **The Civil Rights Act of 1871**, or **The KKK Act,** or **Third Force Act**, was passed in order to curb the outrageous violence of hate groups. This Act *forbade public assembly in costume*; empowered the President to use Federal forces in response; and *it allowed* personal prosecution for violation of constitutional rights. **Note:** *this was later adjusted by the USSC Cases of 1883.*

- **The District of Columbia Organization Act,** defined the territory and governance for this area.

1872 Pinkney Benton Stewart (PBS) Pinchback, of Louisiana, was elected Governor, but only served one month. He was also elected Senator, but was not confirmed. **Note**: *this event is Reconstruction political drama at its most, and would become the issue for Louisiana violence. Please see the entry for the Colfax Courthouse Massacre of April,1873; by the KKK.*

> **Note:** *In 1873, there were seven black representatives, seated in* <u>*the 43rd Congress*</u>. ***Also:***

The Panic of 1873 began a financial depression that lasted 6 years. In the middle of the Reconstruction Era, it caused great resentment towards any progress of blacks.

1873 Bishop Patrick Healy, was the first Black to become president over a predominantly white institution of education. He served from 1873-1881, at Georgetown University.

- ***The Slaughterhouse Cases,*** involved *US Supreme Court rulings*, which limited the protections of the *14th Amendment (citizenship and equal protection)*, by stating that *due process* did not apply to *State* cases (a reversal*). **Note:** far too often the Congress giveth and the Supreme Court taketh away.*
- *The Colfax Courthouse Massacre* occurred on Sunday, April 13th. The KKK attacked the *garrison of the black federal military* who were quartered in Colfax, Louisiana. Between 60-153 were killed. **Note:** *historically, this event has been somewhat overlooked. It represented politics between the black Republicans, and the white supremist Democrats. In retrospect, it represented establishing local power by fear, and political control; as well as the Confederate thumbing its nose at US Amendments, and Acts. Massacres were also a reaction to the increased population of freed slaves. It embodied trends for a future of political tyranny.*

1874 The Coushatta Massacre, by members of the White League of Louisiana, occurred in August. The newly established Parish of *Red River* was run by white "carpetbaggers". The White League seized 6 officials and 4 blacks, and gave them a mock trial. They were killed along with 60–300 Blacks. *The Coushatta Massacre was also a violent reaction to black political involvement.*

- *The Battle at Liberty Place; or the Battle of Canal Street,* occurred In September. This was an *attempted state Coup* by approximately 5,000 White Leaguers. After 3 days, they retreated before the state militia arrived. ***Note:*** *Gov. William Kellogg's* election was *disputed; and new elections were required for Louisiana, because of their continued, and exceptional, political turmoil.*
- *The Freeman's Bank & Trust,* closed on June 29th. It was Established by Congress in 1865, for freed slaves and civil war patriots. It gave hope for financial possibilities to blacks. According to the OCC, *(Office of the Controller of the Currency / US Treasury)* a combination of factors caused its demise; namely, expansion; too little oversight; the Panic of 1873; and inexperience. More than 61,000 depositors, and 3 million in assets were lost with no federal guarantees. ***Note:*** *I believe this created mistrust of banks, for people of color. Frederick Douglas was appointed to save it, but could not.*
- *The Vicksburg Race Riots of 1874,* caused the death of 2 whites, and 29 blacks, in attempts to prevent blacks from voting, and to prevent the return of the town's black mayor, requiring Federal Troops to quell it.

1875 Jim Crow laws were adopted by Tennessee.

- *The Red Shirts* began as a para-military, white supremist group who supported the Democratic Party, by means of terror against black voting, or progress. They were worse than the KKK. *Note: reference the 1921 Black Wall Street Massacre.*
- **The Civil Rights Act of 1875,** was passed, giving blacks the right to public accommodations, and jury duty. **Note:** *Since it did not mandate local or state enforcement, it was ignored.*
- *Blanche Kelso Bruce,* was not the first black Senator, but he was the first to serve a full six-year term in the state of Mississippi.
- **The Mississippi Plan of 1875; or the Shotgun Policy,** was designed to eliminate black Republican involvement in the state.

Note: **The 44th Congress** *had 8 African American Representatives. Also: population disparity in many places directly threatened the political power of supremacists. No matter what social or economic circumstances were, the political circumstances outweighed most other factors. Black participation in the US government would not be tolerated.*

1876 The Hamburg Massacre of South Carolina, occurred in order to prevent blacks from participating in the elections for Governor, and for President.

- **United States v. Rees**e, as the first US Supreme Court ruling after the 15th Amendment, this case determined that US citizens had the right to vote, hold office, and vote without regard to race. It determined that Congress can legislate state elections concerning discrimination.

- *Meharry Medical College* was founded in TN.
- *Jim Crow laws* were enacted in TN.
- **The Civil Rights Act of 1875** guaranteed access to public accommodations, and to jury duty.

Note: The 45th Congress had three black members (5 fewer).

1877 ***The Presidential Election*** between *Samuel J Tilden (D), and Rutherford B. Hays (R),* was hotly contested. The popular vote was won by *Hays,* but *Tilden* had the most *Electoral College* votes. *The Electoral Commission* made a *deal* referred to as *The **Compromise of 1877;*** the liberal Republican *(Hays),* would become President *if* the Democrats agreed to forfeit the EC votes of Florida, South Carolina, and Louisiana. *But Republicans* had to remove all Federal troops from southern states. This gave control of the South to the Democratic (supremacist) right wing, and ended Federal enforcement of Civil Rights legislation.

The Reconstruction Era was brought to a close, *without Federal Support.* **Note:** *alternatives to the popular vote would become a new political tactic regarding Electoral College votes in the next centuries, i.e. the Presidential elections of 1988, 2000, and 2016, and a failed attempt in 2020.*

- *Frederick Douglas,* became the first black US Marshall, appointed by *Pres. Hayes.*

- *Henry O. Flipper,* became the first black to graduate *from West Point Academy.*

1879 Mary Eliza Mahoney, the first professional nurse, graduated from *The New England Hospital for Women.*

> **The Great Migration WEST**, *began, (37 years before the* Great Migration North started). *Benjamin "Pap" Singleton, promoted and encouraged 50,000 African Americans, to migrate from the South, to the West. They were called "The Exodusters; and they settled mostly in Kansas, Missouri, Illinois, and Indiana.* **Also**: *Many all-black towns were created as a result (approx. 60 just in OK). This became an issue in the next century.* **Also**: *the term "Cowboy" is believed to have its origins as a result of this migration (whites were called cow hands). Special mention to Nat Love, Wild Bill Handley, William Preston Longley, and Bass Reeves, etc., cowboys par excellence.*

1880 **Strauder v. West Virginia**, the US Supreme Court ruled that African Americans cannot be excluded from jury duty.

1881 Booker T Washington, founded *Tuskegee Institute, in Alabama;* to promote the education and vocations for black teachers.

- *Spelman College* was founded as the Atlanta Baptist Female Seminary, in the basement of Friendship Baptist Church, *by Harriet Giles, and Sophia Packard.* In 1883, they moved, and changed the name to Spellman, in honor of those related to J.D. Rockefeller, whose support made it possible.

1882 The State Assembly of Virginia, established the Central State Hospital, for mentally-ill African Americans.

Note: Between the years of 1882 and 1928, *approximately 3,445 lynchings occurred.*

1883 **The Civil Rights Cases of 1883,** *t*he Supreme Court ruled that the federal government cannot prevent discrimination; regarding the 5 cases brought to them; as to whether *privately owned businesses* that offered public benefits (i.e. theater, buses etc.) could be held accountable to *the 13ᵗʰ & 14ᵗʰ Amendments, and the Civil Rights Act (of 1875).* **Note:** *this allowed businesses to continue discrimination, and nullified the Civil Rights Acts of 1871 & 1875. Court justice can rewrite law.*

- *The Danville Riot* was a local, politically charged street fight; concerning the liberal *Readjuster Party,* and the white *Democratic Party*. After the death of 4 blacks, the assembly seat in question, and political control, were gained by the white instigators. The racially mixed Readjuster Party *disappeared.*
- **Pace v. Alabama;** *the US Supreme Court* ruled that Alabama's law *against* anti-miscegenation, (or forbidding interracial marriage) was not unconstitutional, *allowing it to remain in place.*

Note: *by the 50ᵗʰ* **Congress there were no black representatives.** *This was the case for about 75 years.*

1884 Judy W Reed, became the first African American woman to receive a patent.

1885 Samuel Davidson, was ordained as a Priest for the Episcopal Church, on June 25th

1886 The Colored Farmers National Alliance was founded in Texas, on December 11th. It was organized to support farmer's issues; and had 5 branches. A cotton workers strike in 1891 most likely led to its demise.

- *The Knights of Labor,* was founded in Philadelphia *because Blacks were excluded from the American Federation of Labor.*
- *Norris Wright Cuney, became the first black chairman of the Texas Republican Party. As an entrepreneur, activist, lawyer, and Freemason; he left a legacy in his state.*

1887 The Thibodaux Massacre occurred on November 23rd, in Louisiana; when *sugar cane workers* attempted to unionize. Approximately sixty were killed. ***Note:*** *this may have been the inspiration for the TV series "Queen Sugar" on the OWN network.*

- *The State Normal School for Coloreds,* was chartered by Congress, as a teacher education facility later known as *Florida A & M* (Agricultural & Mechanical College), an HBCU. ***Note:*** *HBCU is an acronym for Historically Black College or University*
- *Major League Baseball,* prohibited black players. *The Colored Baseball League* was established.

- *Florida* was the first state to legislate *segregation of railroad passengers;* others soon followed.
- *The Afro-American League (AAL) {a precursor to the NAACP},* was founded by journalist, and activist *T. Thomas Fortune.* The first national organization (NAAL), followed in 1890.

1888 Mississippi, legislated to separate railroad passengers.

- *The Capital Savings Bank of Washington, DC.* opened; and remained until 1902.
- *Edward Park Duplex,* was elected in April, as the first black Mayor of a predominantly white town, in Wheatland, CA.

*1889 The Grand Fountain United Order of True Reformers, w*as established as a black fraternal organization which brought about *The True Reformer's Savings Bank; it* received its charter in Virginia, in April.

- *Frederick Douglas,* was appointed as *Minister to Haiti, by Pres., W.H. Harrison.*
- *Florida* instituted a *poll tax* to deter black voters.
- *Virginia State Normal School (University), an HBCU* awarded its first Bachelor Degree.

1890 The 2ⁿᵈ Morrill Land Grant Act was passed (the first one was in 1862}. It provided that states <u>grant lands for higher education facilities for blacks.</u> At present there are 19, A & M Universities

- *Mississippi* enacted literacy and understanding tests, to limit black voting.

- *The Separate Car Act of Louisiana,* was the first state to separate accommodations on railroads. Many states followed suit.
- *Sumner Normal School* was established in St Louis, MO. (later known as Stowe Teachers College; and Harris-Stowe State College).

1891 Provident Hospital, was founded by *Dr. Daniel Hale Williams,* as the first black owned hospital, in Chicago. *Note: In 1893, Dr. Williams performed the first successful open-heart operation (the patient lived 20 years).*

- *West Virginia Colored Institute; Elizabeth State, NC; Delaware State University; and North Carolina A&M,* were all established under the **Land Grant Act** provisions.
- *The National Medical Association* was established by black physicians who were not accepted into the *American Medical Association.*

1892 Ida B Wells, a journalist and activist, began an anti-lunching editorial campaign in Memphis, TN. The lynching death of a friend, whose store was competition for a white business, was her inspiration.

The Stock market crashed in 1893

1893 Henry Smith was arrested, after the death of a police officer's daughter, in Paris, TX. He escaped, was recaptured, and lynched, on Feb 3rd. *Note: What made this extraordinary, was that it became a public event with the attendance of up to 15,000 spectators. He was not hanged; he was tortured and burned alive.* **Also:** *Ida B Wells wrote of this event. It was the original Picnic.*

1894 The Church of God and Christ (COGIC), was founded by Bishop Charles Harrison Mason.

1895 The New Orleans Dock Workers Riot occurred when black, non-union workers were attacked by whites; 6 were killed.

- *Booker T Washington,* delivered his *Atlanta Compromise Address*
- *W E B Du Bois,* received his *PhD from Harvard.*

1896 **Plessy v. Ferguson, the US Supreme Court heard the Louisiana case filed by a railroad; they argued that maintaining the separation of passengers was costly. The USSC ruled to *maintain "separate but equal"*, which justified maintaining segregation, and Jim Crow.

- *George Washington Carver,* became the *Director of Agricultural Research at Tuskegee Inst.* He made great contributions concerning farming and the use of soybeans, peanuts, and sweet potatoes.

1898 The Wilmington Insurrection/ Riot/ Massacre/ & Coup d'etat, of North Carolina. The Republican Fusion (mixed race, liberal) Party had 10 elected officials. *Wilmington, was North Carolina's;* largest city, and was 3/5th black. It was a progressive community. Black entrepreneurs abounded In 1898. It was also an election year for President and for Governor. A *premeditated plan* was established two years in advance, by *The Secret Nine.* Their agenda was to re-establish white supremacy. They created a proclamation named *The White Man's Declaration of Independence.* It established racial hierarchy laws. Their political platform stated *"North*

Carolina, is a white man's state, and white men will rule
It"; we will crush the party of Negro domination so
overwhelmingly, that no other party will ever dare to
attempt to establish Negro rule here. On November 10th,
the culmination of their plans erupted, led by *The Red
Shirts*. The newly elected officials were eliminated by a
mob, representing the *Coup. The massacre* took place the
next day. **Note:** *I have read more than 5 descriptions of
this* <u>state</u> *government take-over. The numbers and the
details vary from 10, to14, to 60, to 300, with thousands
displaced. It was about politics, resentment of the
black/white coalitions, and economics. The massacre
involved 2,000 whites who used a Gatlin gun to rout the
black residents, or as targets, in order to decrease the black
population.* **Note:** *This event perfectly summarized the*
direction and results *of the* **Reconstruction ERA***; an
attempted transition to black freedom that* <u>was limited.</u>

With the end of Reconstruction, *the benchmark was set
for the social-justice directives of our race. The suppression
of blacks remained in place. We will see how US Supreme
Court decisions began to reverse Constitutional Law
intentions.*

**The Spanish American War was declared on April
21, 1898.** *It ended with the Treaty of Paris, signed 4
months later, on Dec 10th. Spain, Cuba, Guam and the
Philippines were at issue. Roosevelt's Rough Riders, and
Buffalo Soldiers, participated. Spanish Colonial territories
of Cuba and the Philippians were ceded to the USA as
part of the treaty. Both wanted their independence. The
Filipinos lost their fight for it. Cuban revolutionaries
ended the matter in 1953.*

1898 **The Louisiana Grandfather Clause (1898-1915),** was enacted to prevent black voters by requiring that a voter's *ancestors* had to be eligible to vote.

1899 ***Cumming v. Richmond City Board of Education*** in GA. In this ruling from the US Supreme Court, concerned the closing of at least 60, overcrowded black high schools; even though the city was building a new white facility. The *"equal"* portion of a previous *separate but equal ruling* was being challenged. Although the Supreme Court ruled in favor of Cumming, the city defied the ruling and maintained the *neglect of educational facilities for blacks.*

The Philippine-American War began *in 1899, and lasted until 1902. The USA would not allow Filipinos to participate in governing themselves. They remained a US Territory until 1946, when their independence was granted.* **Note:** *Buffalo Soldiers served in this war.*

INTRODUCTION TO THE 1900'S

We Fought our fate for the future...

The 1900's were marked by <u>rebellion</u> of all types; even mother nature got involved (the earthquake).

Because there were so many events; my overview of the century is given by quarters:

*The **first quarter,** featured the Street Car Boycott of 1905 - the Great Earthquake of 1906 – WW I - The Spanish Flu Pandemic of 1918 (which ended the war) – lynchings - the beginning of the Great [Migration[s} West and North - and the Wall Street Massacre.*

*The **second quarter,** gave us the Great Stock Market Crash (there were several) the depression, WW II; segregation; and Jim Crow's return; and finally, the elimination of separate but equal (Brown v. Bd of ED, which was the start of something big).*

*The **third quarter was** marked by the Civil Rights Era; and the heroes of the movement are individually listed. YHE War in Vietnam; the assassinations of Pres. JFK - MLK Jr. – Robert Kennedy – Fred Hampton – Malcom X. Many organizations were established to fight for freedoms, along with the FBI's counterintelligence against them. There was no shortage of protests, marches, and mutinies. Add to that, the police killings, (which I consider the same as lynching) and protests concerning them.*

*The **fourth quarter brought** a growing longing for a better quality-of-life. Awareness of economic disparity was on the table; black male imprisonment or unjust legislation was on the table; the dismantling of family life was on the table; along with voting rights, and all manner of Civil Rights,*

*This **century was** a benchmark for inclusion. Great efforts were made by Blacks in the United States, to move the political and social pendulums.*

The 1900's

1900 James W, & John R Johnson, composed the lyrics and music to of the <u>*Negro National Anthem*</u> *"Lift Every Voice & Sing"* to commemorate the birthday *of Abraham Lincoln.*

- *The National Business League,* was founded by *Booker T Washington.*
- *The Robert Charles [New Orleans] Riot, occurred on July 23rd. Charles* shot a white police officer and escaped. The resulting manhunt brought on random shootings and attacks by whites, *with 28 dead and 50 wounded.* There was *international notoriety* over the events. Charles was captured on the 27th.

1901 Booker T Washington, published *"Up From Slavery",* and was invited to dine with Pres. *Theodore Roosevelt,* at the White House. **Note:** *Pres. Roosevelt fought with Buffalo Soldiers in the Spanish American War.*

1902 Jimmy Winkfield, won the Kentucky Derby. In this decade, black jockeys prevailed in horse racing. He also won many races abroad, in Russia, and in France. **Note:** *I'm remembering the story of Jocko Graves, and The Faithful Groomsman.*

1903 W. E. Du Bois, published *The Souls of Black Folks,* regarding the color line in America.

1904 Mary McLeod Bethune, established *Bethune Cookman College,* in Daytona Beach, FL.

- *Sigma Pi Phi,* was established as the first fraternal organization *(outside of Freemasonry)* for African American <u>businessmen</u>; it was not college related.
- *Solomon Carter Fuller,* a pathologist, and professor, *began his body of work with Alois Alzheimer in Europe.* His discovery of the <u>physical impairments</u> common to the mental condition now known as <u>Alzheimer Disease,</u> were groundbreaking. He is still honored in the field of psychology today.

1905 The Nashville Streetcar Boycott, was initiated by *Rev. A. Jones, of St Paul AME Church,* against segregated seating, in TN. It lasted 1 year. By 1906, the *Nashville Transit Co.* went out of business. **Note;** *This was the precursor to the Freedom Rides of the Civil Rights Era, in the 1960's.*

- *The Niagara Movement* for equal rights was held at Niagara Falls, Ontario. *W.E.B. Du Bois and William Trotter* laid the foundation for what would become the *NAACP.*

1906 The Azusa Street Revival began on April 9th, led by *William Seymour.* It set the foundation of the *"Charismatic" or Pentecostal Faith,* in California. **Note:** *one week after the revival, on April 18th, the Great Earthquake of San Francisco,* occurred; *and this made me think of a bible story.*

- *Alpha Phi Alpha, of Cornell University,* is thought to be the first [of many] African American fraternal organizations of higher education.

- *The Brownsville Affair* occurred in Texas, when black soldiers of the *25ᵗʰ Infantry, at Ft. Brown,* were accused of shooting at local homes and businesses. One white bartender was killed. ***Note: President Roosevelt dishonorably discharged 167 black soldiers from the Regiment. They were exonerated in 1970.***
- *Madam C.J. Walker (nee Sara Breedlove), of Louisiana,* established a successful line of hair products for black women. She was known as an activist, and philanthropist.
- *The Atlanta Race Riot,* occurred in Georgia, on Sept. 22ⁿᵈ-24ᵗʰ. With the *usual accusation* of rape, white mobs began random killings of 25-100 black; two whites were also killed. This event was given *international attention.*

The stock market crashed in 1907.

1907 Alain Leroy Locke, was the first African American to become a Rhodes Scholar. He was a philosopher, an author, and was instrumental in the Harlem Renaissance.

1908 The Springfield Race Riots, occurred in Illinois, in August; where more than 1,000 whites raged against blacks for two days, in order to *keep black people in their place.*

1909 **The Sixteenth Amendment to the Constitution,** *established* <u>*Federal Income Taxes.*</u>

- *The NAACP or National Association for the Advancement of Colored People,* was formed; after the Springfield Riot.

- *Matthew Henson, a black explorer,* arrived at the North Pole, along with *Admiral Perry.*
- *The Knights of St. Peter Claver,* were established as the first black *lay Catholic Fraternal Order,* and still exists today.

The Great Migration NORTH began around this time, over the next 4 years.

1910 **Baltimore, MD, designated in City Council* to separate black and white neighborhoods **Note:** *this would be the beginning of REDLING; and was followed by TX, OK, NC, VA, & KY. It became an <u>accepted social standard, and banking practice.</u>*

- *W.E.B. Du Bois,* became the editor of the NAACP's first publication, *Crisis Magazine.*
- *The National Urban League,* was founded by *George Edmund Haynes, and Ruby Standish Baldwin,* in NY. Their goal was to promote jobs, and housing for blacks. It still exists today.

Note: *more than 60 lynchings occurred across the nation in 1912.* **Also:** *One hundred years later, in 2012, more than 48 known police killings occurred; which inspired the <u>Black Lives Matter Movement.</u>*

1913 **The 17th Amendment to the Constitution,** was passed, to designate that a Senator shall be directly elected, by popular vote.

- *Anti-miscegenation laws were in place in 30 states between the years of 1913 and 1948.*

- *Ground breaking, for the Apollo Theater* of New York City, began; it was opened by 1914.
- *Segregation of Federal Facilities* was established by Pres. Woodrow Wilson. **Note**: *Many blacks switched their political party from Republican to Democratic, in order to support him. Wilson made campaign promises for negro advancement. This betrayal was among the factors in the change of liberal blacks from left-wing Republican, to the Democratic Party, in order to support his presidency.*

WORLD WAR I – began on June 28th, 1914

1915 Carter G Woodson, established the *Association for the Study of Negro Life.*

- *The movie, Birth of A Nation, was introduced the white population. It broadened fear and hatred for the black population in its portrayal of black men.*
- **The Oklahoma Grandfather Clause (of 1910),** was ruled as unconstitutional by the US Supreme Court.

1916 Marcus Garvey, arrived in the US. Born in Jamaica, and raised in England; he was an orator. He established the Universal Negro Improvement Association; Black Star Shipping Line, to facilitate the Liberian African Redemption Program; was the publisher of the *Negro World* newspaper in NY. **Note**: *Nearly 100 years previously' Rev. Charles Finley successfully established Liberia, as the original "Back to Africa Movement".*

- *Garrett Morgan,* invented a gas mask, used to rescue men trapped in a tunnel explosion. It was eventually adopted by the US Army.

1917 *The Eighteenth Amendment to the Constitution,* directed the <u>Prohibition </u>of manufacturing of alcohol.

- *The Race Riots of E. St Louis,* occurred in Missouri, between July 2nd – 5th. The rumor of a white man's death exploded into violence. *Actually, i*t was about recent black migrations to the city, and competition for factory work in wartime industry jobs. As many as 200 lives were lost; with extensive property damage; while 6,000 black were <u>*routed from the city.*</u>
- *New York's 5th Avenue* was the location of a march of *a*pproximately *10,000 Blacks,* to protest racial injustice and lynchings, in November.
- *France,* bestowed the *Croix de Guerre (Cross of War),* honoring the foreign service of 107 *black soldiers in WW 1, w*ho were mainly stationed in France, and part of its liberation from Germany.
- *The Houston Riot or the Camp Logan Mutiny,* occurred due to tensions surrounding white police harassment and arrests. Resentment over treatment of the local town's black residents, and the mostly black soldiers at camp, brought a protest march by soldiers during wartime. As a result, there were 110 court martials, with 19 hanged, in August.
- ***Buchanon v. Worley,** six cities or states approved segregated neighborhoods for blacks...*

Only Kentucky's Supreme Court ruled against it, in this case, (see the entry of 1910).

WORLD WAR I ended in November, 1917, *mostly as the result of the Spanish Flu Pandemic.* **Note:** *this Pandemic lasted from February 1918, to April, 1920. It was also a variation of the Coronavirus. This made me understand that the Pandemic of 2020 was not likely to go away in six months, as many believed. The Spanish Flu was thought to have originated in America, and transferred by deploying soldiers.* **Also:** *It was called the Spanish Flu, because Spain was the only country to admit, or report about its existence.*

1918   The South Philadelphia Race Riot, occurred when a mob of approximately 100 angry whites confronted the move-in of a black, to their neighborhood. All were armed; a riot of 3 days ensued**. Note:** *Philadelphia, was, and is, a city of neighborhood boundaries; with as many as 6 riots as proof.*

- *The KKK experienced a rebirth.*

The HARLEM RENAISSANCE, began in 1919, *and lasted until 1931-9. Cultural expressions through music, literature, art, poetry, and dance were prolific during this season of acknowledgement and contributions. Please take the time to look up some of the greats, who had their start at that time, like Zora Neal Hurston, Langston Hughs, etc.*

1919 <u>The Red Summer began</u>. *Nearly 80 blacks were lynched, along with 25 riots across the country. Many of those killed were black veterans, who were unwilling to return to their former status.*

- *Bessie Coleman,* earned her aviation license in France, and returned to America. As a barnstormer, she was known to refuse to perform [in-flight shows] for segregated audiences.
- *The Chicago Riots* occurred on the beaches of Lake Michigan, when Eugene Williams ignored the social requirement of segregation. He was stoned and drowned. This resulted in the death of 15 whites, 23 black, with 1,000 black homes torched. ***Personal Note:*** *now I can understand why my father never let us go on the beach in Atlantic City when I was a child. I though he was just being mean (1950's).*

1920 *The 19th Amendment to the Constitution* was added, which *prohibited the denial to vote,* for any citizen; including women. ***Note:*** *Women's Suffrage succeeded.*

*1921 **The Black Wall St Massacre,** of Tulsa, OK,* occurred between May 31st and June 1st. Some say that a black newspaper article enraged the white population. *The Red Shirts* carried out a two-day rampage that brought about 300 deaths, 6,000 arrests, and 15,000 displaced blacks. The neighborhood, (founded by Ottawa W. Gurley) was bombed, as well as torched (660 businesses, on 4 acres). ***Note:*** *I have reviewed many descriptions of this event. The most informative was an interactive presentation by the New York Times (What the 1921 Tulsa Massacre Destroyed). Over time, the reasons, numbers, and the information, have changed, but the end result did not. The four-block business District of Greenwood was bombed and destroyed; black residents were murdered, detained; and routed. Information about it was actively suppressed.*

- *The Binga State Bank* opened in Chicago, and is said to be the first black owned bank, by Jesse Binga.

1923 The Rosewood Massacre (FL), lasted from January 1 - 7th. It was a series of aggressions carried out by white mobs, attacking residents of this middle-class black town, until it was completely destroyed (*see the movie Rosewood, 1997*).

1924 J. Edgar Hoover, became director *of the FBI, or Federal Bureau of Investigation.* Hoover was an extremist right-winger, who considered any activity for the *Civil Rights of blacks* to be suspicious, subversive, or anti-American. Throughout the many docu-dramas of activists, we see his footprint on our necks.

- *The Cotton Club,* a well-known black entertainment destination, opened in *New York.*
- *Marcus Garvey,* was imprisoned in June, and sent to federal prison for mail fraud. He was released in 1927, and deported to Jamaica.

1925 The National Bar Association, for black lawyers, was established in August, in Des Moines.

- *The Brotherhood of Sleeping Car Porters,* was organized, with A. Philip Randolph, as President. (*see the movie, 10,000 Men Named George, 2002*).
- *The American Negro Labor Congress,* was established, in Chicago, by *A. Philip Randolph.*
- *Dr. Ossian Sweet,* and his brother *Henry Sweet,* had court trials in 1925-6. Dr Sweet purchased a house

in an all-white neighborhood of Detroit. Upon moving in, a mob of 5,000 gathered, and shots were fired in defense. One white, was killed. With the help of the NAACP; and a famous lawyer in their defense, named Clarence Darrow, they won. ***Note: moving forward, this may have inspired the NAACP to change the focus of their efforts to*** <u>*legal issues for black people*</u>.

1926 Carter G. Woodson, initiated the celebration of *Negro History Week, as the 2nd week of February.* ***Note:*** *February, officially became* <u>*Black History Month,*</u> *in 1976.*

1927 The Harlem Globetrotters Team, was formed in Chicago, by Abe Saperstein.

- *Floyd J. Calvin,* became the first black radio talk-show host, and encouraged black activism.
- ***Gong Lum v. Rice****, The US Supreme Court ruled against LUM regarding a case for admittance into a university, because she was Asian. The ruling was that Chinese should be considered as colored. **Note:** This entry was included to demonstrate that blacks were not the only ones who were socially excluded. Asians, and every other ethnic or religious group were discriminated against, and lynched as well. However, their successes did not remain under constant attack.*

1929 The New York City Board of Education, issued a directive that the word Negro, should be spelled with a capital "N" ☺.

THE GREAT STOCK MARKET CRASH, *began in October, 1929; followed by* **The Great Depression**.

Note: *The Depression in the US, (and in the world) seemed to lessen extremist attention. By 1933, Hitler began his rise to power abroad; governments were falling, and tensions were leading towards WWII. In the USA, FDR's New Deal offered relief, but did not bring an end to the* Segregation Era, from 1900-1939.

1930 Wallace Fard Muhammed, founded the *Nation Of Islam [NOI]*, in Detroit. Their approach to black equality was to be self-sufficient, and militant. Four years later, Fard disappeared. *Minister Elijah Muhammed*, who was second in command, assumed leadership until his death in 1975.

1931 Walter White, became the new *Director of the NAACP*, and set its future directive towards *legal battles*.

- *The Scottsboro Boys*, nine black youths were arrested in *Alabama;* with the usual accusation of rape (of two white women). The results of their trials were considered a miscarriage of justice. **Note:** *there were 3 state trials; with two US Supreme Court trials of the individuals over a 6-year period. The survivors spent many years in jail. All were* exonerated by Alabama, in 2013. **Also:** *The notoriety of their plight, and the length of time it took, also helped* set the stage for the coming Civil Rights Era.

1932 The movie *Emperor Jones*, starring *Paul Robeson* was released. **Note:** *Robeson was an activist, athlete,* *lawyer, singer, and actor; who became blacklisted by the FBI.*

- **The Twentieth Amendment to the Constitution** was ratified. It changed the start date of a newly elected President from March, to January, to eliminate the "Lame Duck" session in congress between January and February, after elections.

1933 **The repeal of the 18ᵗʰ Amendment,** *ended* the prohibition of alcohol.

- *The Tuskegee Syphilis Experiment,* began when the *US Public Health Service,* administered the disease, with no treatment or disclosure to the victims. It ended 40 years later. Much later, on May 16, 1997, *Pres. Clinton* gave a formal apology. **Note:** *Among Blacks there is an unspoken mistrust of hospitals and health care, because they were subject to experiments, or lesser care.* **Personal Note:** *My father's father was one of these victims. He was a Minister, and became mentally. It brought shame and quiet whispers to the family.*
- *Carter G Woodson, published the Mis-Education of the Negro, a timely and relevant work.*
- **The 21ˢᵗ Amendment,** *ended Prohibition (of alcohol).*

1934 The Southern Tenant Farmers Union, a bi-racial Socialist Party organization, was formed.

- *Roy Wilkins,* an activist, first became involved with the *NAACP,* as editor of their Crisis Magazine.

*1935 **Norris v. Alabama**;* the US Supreme Court ruled that a jury of your peers is the right of the defendant (*which might automatically include blacks*).

- ***Murrey v. Pearson**; the Maryland Supreme Court ruled African American law students must be admitted to its law school, unless they wished to establish a separate college; they began admitting.*
- *Mary McCloud Bethune, convened 28 leaders from national women's organizations, to form the National Council of Negro Women, in New York.*

1936 Mary McCloud Bethune, was granted a cabinet post in the Roosevelt administration.

- *The NNC or National Negro Congress, was established. A. Phillip Randolf coordinated a wide range of participants; and organizations to effect change, mostly due to the exclusion of blacks, in labor and unions.*
- *Jesse Owens, won 4 gold medals for track & field at the Berlin Olympics. This was significant, considering the times, location, and Hitler.*

1937 After 12 years, the Pullman Company finally signed an agreement with the Brotherhood of Sleeping Car Porters & Maids, to adjust wages and work hours (*see the entry for 1925*).

1938 Dr Charles R Drew pioneered in the separation of red blood cells from blood plasma which saved the lives of many soldiers during the war. He is considered the *father of Blood Banks*. **Note** *at the time, hospitals were segregated and donation of "black" blood was not allowed.*

- *Crystal Bird Fauset,* an activist, became the first black female State Representative in *Philadelphia, PA.*

1939 Billie Holiday, a jazz singer, first recorded *"Strange Fruit"* Her song was a social commentary on lynching, that earned the anger of the FBI; and may have had a factor in her death, 20 years later (*see the movie, United States vs. Billie Holiday, 2021*).

- *Bo Jangles Robinson,* a tap dancer and actor, organized the *Black Actors Guild.*
- *Jane Bolin,* of NY became the first African American *female judge in* the United States.

1940 Actress Hattie McDaniel, became the first black woman to receive an *Oscar,* in her role as Mammy, in the movie *"Gone With The Wind". In a time of segregation, she was not able to participate in the celebrations.*

- *Benjamin O Davis Sr., became the first Afro-American Army General. He was a Rough Rider with Teddy Roosevelt, a Buffalo Soldier and serve on a War committee, advocating for black soldiers.*
- *The NAACP, established the Legal Defense Fund, in keeping with its new directives regarding court cases and laws.*

The **PEARL HARBOR,** *attack on the US Fleet in Hawaii, on Dec. 8, 1941, brought the US into* **WORLD WAR II.** *Japan was at war with China, and this bombing maneuver was their attempt to obtain US oil holdings in the Pacific. Meanwhile; Germany had invaded Poland.*

Although segregated, the military presence and participation of African Americans in WWII was prevalent.

1941   President Roosevelt's Executive Order 8802, desegregated war *defense plants,* and established the Fair Employment Practice Committee.

- *The Double "V", a hand signal,* became popular among black service veterans (from a letter to the Pittsburgh Courier Newspaper, sent by James G Thompson). **Note:** *the first "V" was for victory over the enemy without; the second "V", was for the enemy within. It was their signal.*
- *Dorie Miller,* a Navy cook, in the armed service, was awarded the *Navy Cross,* for his exemplary actions at *Pearl Harbor. A frigate was named for him. In the future, an aircraft carrier will be commissioned in his name between 2026-9.*
- The all-black *Tuskegee Airmen,* known as the *Red Tails, of the US Army,* began training as the 99th Training Squadron. *They saw action, and were honored for their wartime bravery.*
- *The Montford Point [NC] Marines,* were established as a segregated core of black *Marine recruits,* newly allowed to enlist in 1942.
- *Annapolis [MD] Naval Academy,* and other officer training schools, began accepting blacks. *Fort Huachuca, AZ.,* became the recruit training center for *Army males and females.*
- Black Naval seamen manned: *The Destroyer Mason, and PC 1264 during the war.*

- *The Black Panthers, or 761ˢᵗ Tank Battalion,* were part of the *Normandy liberation of France.*
- *George Gibbs reached Antarctica (the South Pole), as part of a Naval expedition. He was the first Afro-American to do so. In 2009, Gibbs Point was named for him.*

1942 The Congress of Racial Equality, or CORE, was founded in Chicago by *six members, James Farmer, George Houser, James R Robinson, Joe Guinn, Homer Jack, and Bernice Fisher.* They would be a strong part of the Civil Rights movement to come.

1943 The Detroit Race Riots at Belle Island Amusement Park, on June 20ᵗʰ, resulted in 700 injured; the death of 25 blacks; and 9 whites, over a 3-day period. A contingent of 6,000 Army troops were needed to quell the riot. ***Note:*** *in 1967 a different riot occurred over the same types of issues, employment, housing racism, etc.*

*1944 **Smith v. Allwright;** t*he US Supreme Court ruled against the right-wing Democratic Party of Texas. Their voter suppression tactic of allowing "white only" candidates in *primary election*s was determined as unconstitutional.

- *The Port Chicago Mutiny (CA),* occurred in July, when black seamen *(not longshoremen)* of the US Navy, refused to continue working on a munitions dock, because of unsafe practices. Previously, conditions caused an explosion of the *SS E A. Bryan; and the death of 300+, with 400 injured. Thurgood Marshall w*as instrumental in overturning the wrongful conviction of mutiny for the Chicago 50, who were exonerated in 1946.

- *The Freeman Field Mutiny* occurred on April 4th-5th, in *Seymour, IN.* *The black officers of the 477th Bombardment Group,* attempted to integrate the white *Officer's Club at Freeman Army Airfield (read the Guard of Honor, 1949; a Pulitzer Prize winning novel of the event).*

President Franklin D. Roosevelt died on April 12th.

1945 The United Nations, a worldwide organization for peace and security, was founded on October 24th.

- *Ebony Magazine, w*as published by *John H. Johnson.* Black owned, it featured full articles of the Who's-Who, for the national black community.
- *Colonel Benjamin O Davis Jr,* became the first black military Base Commander, at Goodman Field, Kentucky. Like his father, he was an advocate for Black servicemen, and established the Tuskegee Airman. He was instrumental in desegregating the Air Force in 1948. ***Personal Note:*** *my uncle served under him in the Korean War (1950-1953).*
- *The Six Triple Eight Postal Directory Battalion was an all-black female unit deployed to Europe in February, to accomplish delivery of a three-year backlog of mail. It boosted the morale of soldiers, and relief for loved ones.*

WORLD WAR II, ENDED on Sept 2, 1945, *Germany, and Japan surrendered.* ***Note:*** *after the war, Southerners* *or Supremacists again expected black soldiers to accept the social status-quo. However, black veterans were not willing to go along with it. Many vets were victimized (much like in the Red Summer of 1919, after WW I). This time, their answer was to rebel. Also, according to the Smithsonian Magazine, membership in the NAACP grew from 50,000 to 450,00. The makings of a movement were in place.* <u>*The new battlefront was state opposition to voting; integration; and education for blacks.*</u>

- *Adam Clayton Powell Jr. [NY)* the former pastor of Abyssinian Baptist Church, was elected to the *House of Representatives,* (he served three terms). He was *controversial* concerning his involvement with the civil rights movement; and [later], his seat in congress in 1969.

1946 **The Employment Act of 1946,** *President Trueman's* initiative stated that all person's ready and able to work, should be able to do so. The Act, established agencies and actions that are still in practice today.

- *Dr. Charles H Johnson,* became the first black President of *Fisk University [TN], an HBCU.*
- *Paul Robeson, (see the 1932 entry),* founded the *American Crusade Against Lynching.*
- **Morgan v. Virginia,** *the US Supreme Court ruled that segregation in interstate bus travel was unconstitutional.* **Note:** *Interstate commerce is within federal jurisdiction.*

1947 <u>*The Journey of Reconciliation*</u>, was the name given to the first *Freedom Ride.* Sixteen interracial members of

CORE, including the organizer *Bayard Rustin,* took a dangerous bus tour across 6 states in the South. (*see the Netflix movie - Rustin, 2023*).

- *Jackie Robinson,* integrated *American League Baseball*
- *John H Franklin* published a black history textbook, *From Slavery to Freedom.*

1948 Pres. Harry Truman, gave *Executive Order # 9981* to desegregate the military, three years after the war ended.

- *Alice Coleman,* was the first black female *Olympic Medalist, in France.*
- **Shelly v. Kraemer,** *the US Supreme Court* ruled that it could not mandate racial restrictions, specifically regarding the sale of *housing to non-Caucasians;* this was the jurisdiction of the state.
- **Perez v. Sharp***; the California Supreme Court,* ruled to allow interracial marriage.
  Note: *this should not be confused with the USSC ruling of 1967.*
- *Timmie Rogers* began the first black TV show, *Sugar Hill Times,* on CBS-TV. It also featured Willie Bryant, Thelma Carpenter, and Harry Belafonte.

1949 WERD-AM, the first black owned radio station began and was programed by Jesse Blayton, in *Atlanta, GA.*

- *Harvard University* had its first black professor, *Dr. William A Hinton.*

- *Annapolis Naval Academy,* graduated its first black, *Commander Wesley A Brown.*

The 1949 Housing Act, and Urban Renewal Program, supported the concept of *"The Projects"* as a housing solution for *the segregated urban blacks.* **Note: *this is also the time when urban street gangs became popular among blacks.*

> **After the War, Jim Crow was revived,** *to decrease post war job competition. When television, (which originated in 1928), became a household item; the fight and protests for black inclusion reached higher heights, through greater awareness. The McCarthy Era, and black-listing came into being. The FBI gathered intelligence on civil rights activists. Several artists of the Harlem Renaissance left the country and continued their activism from abroad (i.e. author James Balwin, dancer Josephine Baker, singer Eartha Kit, etc.*

1950 Gwendolyn Brooks, received the *first Pulitzer Prize* given to an *African American, for poetry.* She was most noted for the poems *Annie Ellen,* and later, *We Real Cool.*

- *Ralph Bunch, of the United Nations,* won the *Nobel Prize for Peace,* as mediator between Arab and Israeli disputes. In 1963, he received the *Medal of Freedom* from Pres. Kennedy.
- The NBA, or National Basketball Association *was integrated by Earl Lloyd, Chuck Cooper,* and *Nathaniel Clifton.*

- *The Tony Award (on Broadway)* was awarded to the first black; *Juanita Hill, for South Pacific.*
- *"The Banker",* a movie about Bernard Garrett and Joe Morris, was released in 2020, it gave a true portrayal of the banking and real estate dealings of two black men in the 1950 -60's, when Jim Crow was in place.

*1951 **The 22nd Amendment**,* limited the maximum Presidential term office to *8 years, or two terms.*

- *Henrietta Lack's* blood cells became *"immortal"* when her cancer cells lived outside her body. Samples were taken by *Dr. Gey* of *Johns Hopkins Medical Center.* The *HeLa blood samples* continue to be a source of medical research today. ***Note:*** *no compensation to her family was ever made. Disclosure did not occur until 1975.*
- *JET Magazine,* owned and published by *John H. Johnson,* was introduced as a weekly pocket-sized summary of black social and entertainment happenings. ***Note:*** *Later, Jet received national recognition for an article with pictures concerning the death of Emmett Till.*
- *Harry T Moore, and his wife Harriett,* died from injuries received, after a bomb under their bedroom, exploded. Moore and his wife were educators; he established the Florida NAACP. *It is assumed that the KKK was involved. This is the only instance where husband and wife were murdered.*

*1953 **District of Columbia v. John R Thompson**, the* US Supreme Court heard this case brought against Johnson, whose restaurant would not serve *Mary Terrell.* It was also about segregation in DC., housing, education, and business. Howard Law School helped to devise the case, which they won, on the grounds of the ***Organic Act of 1878** (requiring only Congress could legislate DC.).*

- *Minnie Jocelyn Elders, was appointed Surgeon General of the US, by Pres. Clinton.*

*1954 *****Brown v. Board of Education of Topeka, KS,*** was a landmark decision concerning segregation of *(or separate schools)*. The US Supreme court ruled that it was unconstitutional. There was a total of 5 cases that cleared a path for the longed-for change. ***Note:** Thurgood Marshall, Dir. of the NAACP Legal Defense Fund, was instrumental. **Also:** this case reversed the USSC decision of Plessy v. Ferguson which proposed "separate but equal" segregation (that never happened). **Personal Note:** my own education started at an all-black elementary school, which is probably why I had so many questions, and disliked history so much.*

- *Malcolm X, became Minister of Temple #7, Nation of Islam (NOI), in New York.*
- *Benjamin Oliver Davis Jr., of the Air Force, was appointed to be the first black Brigadier General, as well as the first black Commander of an airbase, by Pres. Eisenhower.*
- ***Hernandez v. Texas,** again the 14th Amendment <u>was upheld</u> by The US Supreme Court, to provide* equal protection under the law, regarding jury

selection; and the inclusion of *Mexican Americans*. *Note: this case advanced the civil rights of all minorities.*

- ***Davis et al v. the St Louis Housing Authority;*** the state court of *Missouri* heard the class-action suit against St Louis, for the discrimination between applicants and placements in public housing. Civil Rights attorney *Frankie Muse Freeman, of the NAACP, won her case.*

1955 Emmett Till, a 14-year-old from Chicago, was tortured and killed in *Money, MS.* on August 28th. He was accused of making advances towards a white female grocery clerk, while visiting relatives for the summer. ***Note:*** *pictures of the open casket, published in Jet Magazine, sent shock waves across the nation.* ***Personal Note:*** *sending your kids to relatives for the summer was a common practice at that time. Like Emmett's visit South, I didn't understand about segregation, and didn't know why they wouldn't serve me a soda at the Maryland bus station. We lived in our own little bubble.*

1956 ***Browder v. Gayle;*** Claudette Colvin, and 5 others were the plaintiffs in a lawsuit against segregation on Alabama's bus transportation. The original incident happened in Dec.,1955, when Ms. Colvin, (a teenager who was with child), would not give up her seat to a white passenger. ***Note:*** *The incident got the attention of MLK Jr. who decided to do a retake of the event, and make it count.* ***Also:*** *the actual first refusal to give up a seat (on an interstate bus trip) was by Pauli Murray, in 1940.*

- *Autherine Lucy Foster, a young* activist, attempted to enroll at University of Alabama. Her acceptance was rescinded. With the help of the NAACP, *Thurgood Marshall, and the 1956 ruling;* her 3-year effort and court case were won. In Feb. she attended her first class; after riots broke out, she was expelled. ***Note:*** *years later, she returned to graduate.*
- <u>*Rosa Parks,*</u> *refused to move to the back of the bus, in Dec.,1955.* She was arrested in Montgomery [AL}; (as planned by the local NAACP: *Ms. Parks was* their secretary*). The Women's Political Council* suggested a boycott which MLK Jr. agreed to. It was organized, and lasted 381 days. The bus company went out of business, in the end. ***Note:*** *TV helped to galvanize efforts for change, as the freedom movement took shape. This incident was a key part of it. Ms. Park's courage has been honored nationally.*
- <u>*The Counter Intelligence Program,*</u> *or* COINTELPRO *was organized by the FBI, and* remained in place until 1971. It proceeded to gather information on the *Civil Rights Movement,* and any activists; to derail; neutralize; dismantle; or otherwise stop civil activists' progress. Their *actions included surveillance infiltration, informants, fake news, police harassment, spies, and other aggressive actions.* ***Note:*** *the docu-drama Judas and the Black Messiah, 2021, is a prime example.* ***Also:*** *As part of that program, legalized killing by "authority" became a suppression tactic.*

- *The Mississippi State Sovereignty Commission* was established so that *Governors* could *deter integration,* and manage civil rights activism; it lasted until 1973.
- *Singer Nat King Cole,* was assaulted onstage in April. In November, he hosted a prime-time variety show for NBC. It was canceled because sponsors feared to support the show in a time of segregation.
- **The Southern Manifesto,** was created by *Congressman Strom Thurmond Sr. [SC],* and *Richard Russell.* It represented the extreme right-wing, and opposed the racial integration allowed by the *Browder v. Gale, USSC ruling.*

1957 The Southern Christian Leadership Conference, or SCLC, was founded by *Rev. Martin Luther King Jr.,* to promote equality. *This transitioned him to a fuller social commitment,* (in addition to church). From here, he was able to bring together organizations and talented influentials, towards civil rights goals. As a gifted orator, he was the "kingpin" that *moved the movement (read King A Life, 2023).* **Note:** *you may observe that many of the Civil Rights leaders were former ministers. Consider that they could INSPIRE and deliver a message to a wide audience (before the internet).*

- **The Civil Rights Act of 1957**, *Pres. Eisenhower,* established the *Civil Rights Commission* for the *Justice Dept.* and authorized it to prosecute voting rights violations. **Note:** *legislation for this Act brought on the longest filibuster in the Senate's history, by Strom Thurmond (See the Southern manifesto of 1956).*

- *Pres. Eisenhower sent* Federal Troops to *Arkansas,* to confront State Troopers, *ordered by Gov. Faubus,* and to prevent rioting at *Little Rock's Central High School, as 9 black children* came to integrate the school, in September. ***Note:*** *this was a test of the Brown v. Bd of Ed. ruling.*
- *The Little Rock 9,* were students who attempted to integrate Central High School of MS. This was a test of the Brown v. Bd of Ed ruling of 1954. They were denied admission, but later attended with the intervention of Pres. Eisenhower.

1958 MLK Jr. experienced a failed assassination attempt on his life, on Sept 20th in *Harlem, NY.*

1959 John Howard Morrow was appointed Ambassador to Guinea. He was also a linguistics professor at several colleges.

The Civil Rights Movement was in full effect in the 1960's. It was powered by a Supreme Court Ruling.

1960 **Boynton v. Virginia,** the US Supreme Court ruled that *Boynton* was not trespassing, by sitting in the "Whites Only" section of <u>a bus terminal.</u> ***Note:*** *regarding interstate transportation facilities.*

- *SNCC, or Student Nonviolent Coordinating Committee,* initiated *SIT INS,* as 4 college students were refused service at Woolworth's lunch counter, in Greensboro, NC. *This effort was well organized, interracial, peaceful, and <u>televised.</u>*
- **Rep. Julian Bond,** – a native of *Atlanta, GA.* was a co-creator of the Student Nonviolent Co-

ordinating Committee (SNCC) in 1960; a key group of the Civil Rights Era. By 1965 he won election to the Georgia House of Rep. but was not seated until 1967 via US Supreme Court order. He later became Communications Director for the National NAACP (1998-2010). His favored quote was "Good things don't come to those wait; it comes to those who agitate".

- *Gomillion v. Lightfoot* was a landmark decision concerning Gerrymandering, a common state practice. This USSC ruling determined that manipulating district boundaries to limit electoral college voter representation by race, violated the 15th Amendment. **Note:** *more recently, states have manipulated around this ruling by determining boundaries according to political affiliation.*

"Women's Liberation" became a national movement over the next 20 years.

1961 "Freedom Rides" began on May 7th, by *C.O.R.E.* Over a span of 5 months and 5 states, freedom riders enabled the desegregation of bus terminals; an effort that began as early as 1947. The involvement of *John Lewis* and 12 others, *plus Attorney General Robert F. Kennedy, President John F Kennedy, the Supreme Court, the NAACP and SNCC supported.* White mob violence met them. Riders were jailed, beaten, and a bus was bombed.

- The movie *Hidden Figures (2016)*, depicts the story of 3 black female mathematicians who made the space orbit of astronaut John Glenn, possible in

1962; *Mary Jackson, Dorothy Vaughn, and Katherine Johnson.*

- **The 23rd Amendment** allowed voting privileges to residents of *Washington, DC,* in presidential elections, and provided them 1 vote in the Electoral College.

- **Rep. John Lewis,** an ordained Baptist Minister, first became an activist with the Sit-Ins in Nashville; and then the Freedom Rides of 1961. He was one of the *"Big 6"*. In the *March* on *Washington* in *1963,* he was most noted for his participation on *Bloody Sunday,* on the march across the *Edmund Pettus Bridge,* in *AL.* He was also part of the *Freedom Summer Movement* for voter registration of *1964.* In *1987* he became a statesman and served in the *House of Representatives for Georgia from 1987 – 2020.* In *1988,* he introduced a bill to establish *a National African American Museum of History and Culture,* which was realized under *Pres. George W Bush,* and opened in 2016. He was also noted for encouraging people to *"Get into Good Trouble",* concerning Activism.

- *James Farmer –* was a co-founder of *CORE, the Congress Of Racial Equality,* and served as its chairman from *1942 to 1944.* He was the originator of the term *"Freedom Rides".* Courts ruled that segregation was unconstitutional; *in the cases of Morgan v. Commonwealth - 1946,* and in the *Boynton v. Virginia – 1960.* However, bus segregation remained in southern states. *In May of 1961, Freedom Rides* began to challenge these states. Farmer was considered one of the *"Big 6".* and part of the *March on Washington.*

- *Vernon E Jordan Jr. Esq.* – a native of *Atlanta, GA.* and graduate of *Howard Law School* - sued the *University of Georgia in Federal Court,* victoriously; providing admission of black students to the university. He continued as an activist with the *NAACP; National Urban League;* and advisor to *Presidents Carter and Clinton.*

1962 James Meredith - was denied Admission to *University of Mississippi.* He filed suit with the US District Court on May 31st (with aid of the NAACP); which ruled in his favor. On Sept. 30th there is a riot, with 2 killed and 300 injured. On Oct 1st, Meredith was escorted by US Marshals. *Attorney General Robert Kennedy* intervened with *Governor Ross Barnette.* Meredith was the first black ever to attend *(and graduate)* "Ole Miss".

1962 **Bailey v. Peterson,** this case was heard by the USSC regarding segregation on interstate travel. The case was returned, for jurisdiction at lower levels.

- *Fannie Lou Hamer* attended a voter registration rally in Mississippi, and the rest is history. She became a powerful and persistent activist for voting rights and economic opportunities. Her most noted statement was: "I'm sick and tired of being sick and tired".

1963 April 16, 1963, MLK Jr wrote his *"Letter from a Birmingham Jail"* in response to white clergy.

- *The Birmingham Children's Crusade* occurred *May 2-5.* On the first day of the first March, about 800 children left school and convened at the *16ᵗʰ Street Baptist Church*, led by *Rev James Bevel* of SCLC. *On the second day* they were met by" police dogs, and fire hoses. MLK Jr. and others joined their cause to desegregate the shopping district in Alabama. *Bull Conner* left office on May 10ᵗʰ, as part of his negotiations for an end.
- *Medgar Evers, the Field Secretary of NAACP* was _assassinated_ on July 2ⁿᵈ at his home in Mississippi. He was a dedicated activist, involved with issues regarding Emmett Till, James Meredith, and voting rights. *Byron de la Beckwit*h was accused. After 3 trials, and 31 years later, he was convicted in 1994.
- *The March on Washington* occurred on August 28ᵗʰ. Organized by *Martin Luther King Jr and A. Phillip Randolph.* A gathering of approximately 250,000 (?) came to promote economic and civil change. MLK Jr. delivered his famous *"I Have A Dream"* speech.
- The bombing of *the 16ᵗʰ Street Baptist Church* happened in Birmingham; AL. The attack caused the death of 4 young black girls, and injured 22, on September 15ᵗʰ.
- *President John F Kennedy* was _assassinated_ in Dallas, TX. on November 22ⁿᵈ. The loss was profound among blacks; we considered him friendly

to our causes, and "one of us". It was also considered a *coup d'état, by many.*

1964 The Freedom Summer Movement began in June. For 10 weeks many converged to register black voters, who were disenfranchised for years, in *Mississippi.* Efforts were coordinated from *SNCC, CORE, SCLC, NAACP, ACLU, National Assoc. of Churches with out of state white volunteers, the National Lawyers Guild, and many more.* The movement experienced 8 murders, mobs, and beatings; with bombings of homes, businesses, and churches. *Hard core MS residents and the KKK resisted vehemently.* The nation was horrified to learn of the murders *of Michael Schwerner, Andrew Goodman (both white) from NY, and James Cheney* as part of the *Freedom Summer* deaths. ***Note:*** *also named as the Mississippi Burning Murders*

- The ***Civil Rights Act of 1964*** *was signed by President Linden B Johnson on July 2nd,* addressing discrimination by race, color, religion, sex or national origin; also, labor laws.
- ***The 24th Amendment*** *prohibited Poll Taxes and Literacy Tests, regarding voting.*
- ***The Food Stamp Act*** *or Supplemental Nutrition Assistance Program (SNAP)* was established as part of President Johnson's *War on Poverty and still exists today.*
- *Martin Luther King Jr.* was awarded the *Nobel Prize for Peace,* on December 10th

The US officially became involved in the WAR IN VIETNAM IN 1965; it ended in 1975. Over the course

of the war, black soldiers were disproportionately higher (14%), than in the US population (11%), while facing discrimination in the military. Civil Rights complaints about the death ratios for black soldiers inspired Presidential (LBJ) intervention to decrease it.

1965   The Moynihan report of 1965 brought the issue of the black family to the forefront. *Between 1970- 75, Welfare Mothers became a social issue. The deterioration of the black family was abetted by social requirements for assistance, and the lack of jobs for black men (see the movie Claudine - 1974). It became a campaign issue for Pres. Reagan in 1976, when the tag of "Welfare Queen" was presumed for all who needed assistance. The Rockefeller Drug Laws, the privatization of prisons, and the war, also helped to contribute to absentee fatherhood among Black men. Adjustments to the Welfare system were also promoted by Pres. Clinton's reform Act as a deterrent to generational dependency.*

- *Malcolm X* was <u>*assassinated*</u> on February 21st. As an Islamic activist and orator, he believed the black man should *create his own economic freedom and autonomy.*
- *Jimmy Lee Jackson,* an activist with SCLC *was* at a protest rally on Feb. 18th to prevent the possible lynching of James Orange. He, and others fled into a restaurant, they were pursued and he was shot in the stomach by State Trooper James Fowler, after the protest. A visit with him at the hospital, from MLK Jr., inspired the *Bloody Sunday March. Jackson died* from the gunshot wound.

- *Bloody Sunday* occurred in Selma, AL, on the *Edmund Pettus Bridge,* as voting rights marchers were met by police with dogs, water hoses and attacked, *on March 7th The nation watched the events on TV. Two weeks later, another march occurred on March 24th from Selma to Montgomery (54 miles). For 5 days, this interracial group of 25 thousand had the protection of Federalized troops, ordered by Pres. LBJ.*
- **The Voting Rights Act of 1965** were passed on August 6th. It restored the 15th Amendment rights, and reversed the effects of the *Supreme Court ruling of 1883.* It also outlawed *prohibitive* state and local requirements to vote.
- *Race Riots of Watts, Los Angeles* began on August 11th and lasted 5 days. The igniting incident concerned a traffic stop. Great tension, fueled by economic deprivation, overcrowding, and unemployment, exploded with looting, 34 deaths, and 1,032 injured; with more than 3,000 arrests.
- **The Hart-Cellar Act** – eliminated *immigration quotas* that were established in 1952.

1966 Stokely Carmicheal, a former philosophy student at Howard University, was a member of SNCC; and a community activist. He was most known for his rally speech for *"Black Power" inspiring the Nashville Riot.* A Movement began. The phrase had a different meaning for different people. His *revolutionary rhetoric* and sympathies towards the Black Panthers, created danger from the FBI.

- *Huey Newton, and Bobby Seale organized the "Black Panther Party";* originally a community grass roots organization for the poor. It became a threat for its armed and militant stance against white supremacy. S. Carmichael was also part of this group.
- *KWANZAA* was introduced as a 7-day cultural celebration of principles for black people, by *Dr. Maulana R Karenga.*
- *Rev. Dr. Pauli Murray, a professor, activist, lawyer, author, co-founded the National Organization of Women (NOW) along with Betty Friedman, Shirley Chisholm, and Muriel Fox.* As a social justice advocate, and *legal advisor* to leaders of the civil rights movement; she fought for education; women's rights, gender equality; and often *identified* as <u>she</u>. *(see the documentary, My Name is Pauli Murray, 2021).*

*1967 **The 25th Amendment*** described the process by which a President is replaced.

- *Thurgood Marshall* was seated as the first African American Justice of the US Supreme Court. He served until 1991. As a civil rights activist, and legal counsel to the NAACP he was best known for his involvement with the case of Brown v. Board of Education of (KS) 1964 (school desegregation).
- *The Long Hot Summer"* describes this season of discontent marked with <u>159 Riots</u> across the US, as whites continued their exodus to suburbia. Economic conditions (unemployment, overcrowding,

poverty, police practices, redlining, banking discrimination, etc. etc.) boiled over into protests.

- **Loving v. Virginia,** *the Supreme Court ruled that laws in VA. against interracial marriage were* <u>*unconstitutional*</u>*. The ruling was a landmark for anti-miscegenation laws nationwide.*
- *The Philadelphia Plan* was established as an affirmative action plan to include minority *construction contractors* on Federal projects.

1968 The Orangeburg Massacre occurred on Feb 8th as State Troopers opened fire on *200 students* while protesting segregation at *South Carolina University;* 28 wounded, 3 killed.

- ***Jones v. Alfred H Meyer Co.*** was heard by the USSC, and determined that *Congress* could regulate the sale of private property, and discrimination in sales, regarding the Civil Rights Acts.
- *MLK Jr.* delivered his famous speech, *"I've been to the Mountain-Top" at Mason Temple in Memphis, TN., on April 3rd.*
- *Martin Luther King Jr.* was <u>assassinate</u>d on April 4th, In Memphis, TN. **Note:** *At the time of his death, MLK Jr. had refocused his efforts towards the poor and disenfranchised of all colors, not just black people. His belief that the money spent on the War in Vietnam could be better spent on the impoverished, which earned him great disfavor.*
- *The Holy Week Uprisings,* brought over <u>*100 Race Riots*</u> after *the death of MLK Jr.,* in many major cities and ghettos.

***The Fair Housing Act** or **Title 8 of the Civil Rights
Act of 1968*** was signed April 11th by President Lyndon
Johnson, creating *HUD or The Department of Housing
and Urban Development*. This Act gave recourse to those
experiencing housing discrimination, but there was *no
means, method, or penalties to enforce it*. According to the
Chicago Tribune, *modern day redlining still exists*.

- *Shirley Chisholm (of NY)* was elected to the House
  of Representatives as the first black female ever to
  do so.
- *The Poor Man's March* occurred on May 12th. The
  March and the *Campaign* were planned by
  MLK Jr. of SCLC. After his death, it was led by
  Ralph Abernathy. It concerned the economic
  disparity of all persons. The Campaign
  established *Resurrection City* on the
  Washington Mall for six weeks with
  approximately 3,000 participants The
  Campaign established *Resurrection City* on the
  Washington Mall for six weeks with
  approximately 3,000 participants. **Note:** *I believe
  that Operation COINTELPRO was in action to
  disenfranchise this program.* **Note:** *Around this
  time, places like Mississippi actually had food
  embargos for those who wanted to vote. King,
  knew that poor people of all races were starving
  in places like the South, and Appalachia.* **Also:**
  *Some of the results accomplished later were
  Operation Head Start, lunch programs, summer
  jobs programs, the Bureau of Indian Affairs,
  and many coalitions for human rights of all*

disadvantaged races, and religions.

- *Senator Robert F Kennedy, the Presidential* candidate, and former *Attorney General* was <u>*assassinated*</u> on June 5th. The hope for black causes was greatly affected also.
- *Tommie Smith and John Carlos* held their fists up (the Black Power salute) in a show of solidarity and protest at the Olympic Awards Ceremony. They were stripped of their medals, and not allowed to return. **Note:** *the more current "taking a knee", or any other idea of protest usually gathers more attention than the* reason *for it.*
- **Powe v. Miles** the Supreme Court ruled that *educational institutions* receiving any *federal funding* are held to the *Civil Rights Act,* regarding admissions and treatment of students.
- **Batson v. Kentucky** ruled that no potential juror can be peremptorily excluded (decided upon) based solely on race, regarding *equal protection under the law.*

1969 The Congressional Black Caucus was established.

- *Students at Brandeis, University of Wisconsin, Duke, Cornell, Colgate, and New York City colleges* protested to *demand* black study courses on their campus.
- *Race Riots* occurred in *Hartford, CT* concerning economic conditions; and *in Camden, NJ* concerning police brutality.
- *Fred Hampton, of the Black Panther Party, was killed* as part of a police raid on his apartment.

- *The Revised Philadelphia Plan* allowed that *affirmative action quotas were against the Civil Rights Act, making compliance voluntary* in order to appease the blue-collar resistance to including black contractors.

- ***Terry v. Ohio,*** concerned the *police policy of "Stop & Frisk".* The US Supreme Court ruled that a stop was *not unreasonable* <u>even when there was *no "probable cause".*</u> They stated that *reasonable suspicion* was acceptable, for police actions. **Note:** *The "Terry Stop" justified the beginning of a policing nightmare for Blacks. This is the first of three USSC rulings that gave police <u>zero accountability</u> (immunity), to shoot first, and ask questions later.* **Note:** <u>*The question of "what did I do wrong?" became MOOT.*</u> *The cases of Brown v. Texas, and Whren v. US, are related to this decision.*

- *Rev. Al Sharpton,* began a lifetime of activism, as head of *Operation Bread Basket (sponsored by Rev. Jesse Jackson).* He headed many protest marches after police killings, and coined the phrase *No Justice, No Peace!* He later founded *the National Action Network in 2004,* and is currently a featured commentator on *MSNBC News.*

- *The Ford Foundation,* allotted money to fund Afro-American history courses *at Yale, Howard, and Morgan State Universities. Harvard also* established a program named for W E B Du Bois. (Harvard's program was protested).

- *Bowdoin College, an abolitionist citadel* of Afro-American support for two centuries, established an Afro-Americans studies course.

- *Hartford, CT.,* experienced a race riot, concerning economic conditions. *Camden, NJ.* experienced a riot concerning police brutality.
- *Moneta Sleet Jr.,* won the Pulitzer Prize, for his photo of *Coretta King, the widow of MLK Jr.,* in Ebony Magazine in 1969.
- *Jimmy Hendrix* was the headline performer at *Woodstock,* the world's largest musical outdoor festival, in August.
- Freedom Bank & Finance opened in Los Angeles, headed by Venable F Booker. His bank did not fail, and he sold it upon retiring years later.
- *Fred Hampton, and Mark Clarke, of the Black Panther Party,* were slaughtered in a pre-dawn police raid in Chicago, on Dec. 4th.

THE CIVIL RIGHTS ERA ENDED

1970 Dr. Clifton Wharton Jr, became the first black President *of Michigan State University.* **Note:** *this entry should not be confused with the Wharton School of Business, at Penn State Univ.*

- *The Congressional Black Caucus* was established in the *House of Representatives.*
- *The Chicago 7,* were acquitted of charges against them, regarding a plot to disrupt the *1968 Democratic National Convention.* Among the protesters against the War in Vietnam, Bobby

Seale (of the Black Panthers), was included with them *in error*. A fact that the judge attempted to ignore. (see the movie The Chicago 7, 2020).

- *Essence Magazine, and Black Enterprise Magazine* was published by Edward Lewis, Clarence O. Smith, Cecil Hollingsworth, and Jonathan Blount.
- *The NAACP, successfully campaigned against President Nixon's nominee as a Justice* for the Supreme Court. *G H Carswell* a known right-wing extremist, was defeated.
- *Charles Gordone,* won the *Pulitzer Prize* for his play *"No Place to Be Somebody" in 1970.*
- *The Soledad Brothers;* were activists who wrote about, and fought for *awareness of extreme cruelty and racism, in Soledad California State Prison.* Their fight drew worldwide attention *(re: the 8th Amendment).* They were on the FBI's 10 most wanted list.
- *The Marin County Courthouse Incident,* involved black armed guards, who attempted to free the *Soledad Brother*s, at their court appearance*. Note: It was believed* that *Angela Davis, (a former Black Panther supporter and former activist with socialist equality beliefs)* was involved with this incident. Four were killed, including the judge, in August. She was exonerated later.
- *Eddie Conway, the Marshall of Baltimore's Black Panther Party,* was accused of police murder. He was arrested; convicted (considered as a political prisoner), and imprisoned for 44 years. (also see Mumia Abu Jamal).

- *Jackson State University,* and *Kent State University,* both experienced death by police authority in May:
- *At Jackson State MS, (an HBCU),* police opened fire on students gathered outside a dormitory at midnight. Two were killed. Phillip L Gibbs, and James E. Green.
- *At Kent State University,* students protested the War in Vietnam. The Ohio National Guard opened fire on the gathering; 4 were killed, and 9 were wounded.
- **Bob Jones University v. The United States;** in this case, the tax-exempt status of BJU was challenged. It took 17 years to resolve (until 1983), and they lost their exemption as a religious institution under Title 9, *because they would not admit black students.*

1971 Swann v. Charlotte-Mecklenburg Board of Education (SC), the US Supreme Court ruled that busing children to integrate schools was an appropriate solution to the geographic problem. **Note:** *this affected school populations for the next 20 years.*

- *Angela Davis,* had her day in court, and was *exonerated* by the state of California, on June 9th. **Note:** *she was also targeted by the FBI as an activist with sympathies for the Black Panthers.*
- *The Attica Prison Riot / Uprising* occurred between Sept 9th to 13th. Half of *New York's State Prison* population protested their inhumane treatment, and conditions. *Gov. Rockefeller* refused to enter negotiations. Instead, he sent enforcements to quell

the uprising; resulting in the death of 10 officers, and 33 inmates.

- *Rev. Jesse Jackson,* established *PUSH, {People United to Save Humanity).* He was active with SCLC, along with MLK Jr.; and the Civil Rights Movement of the 60's. Later, he created the Rainbow Coalition for his Presidential campaigns of 1984 and 1988. He also became a foreign envoy for Pres. Clinton.

- *Leroy "Satchel" Page,* of the former *Negro Baseball League,* was inducted into the *Baseball Hall of Fame*; *Beverly Johnson*, became the first black female on the cover of *Glamour Magazine;* black owned *Johnson Products*, was listed on the AMEX, NY Stock Exchange.

- **Reed v. Reed***;* the USSC voted to strike down any legislation which did not provide equal protection under the law, for women also. **Note:** *Justice RBG was involved in this issue.*

- The federal government officially ended the FBI's covert intelligence gathering program, COINTELPRO or Counterintelligence Program. **Note:** *This program is credited with the death of 28 Blank Panther Party members, and the imprisonment of 750 persons.* **Also:** *a Congressional inquiry determined that the program was a violation of rights. Nothing was done concerning the victims.*

1972 Barbara Jordan (TX), and *Andrew Young (GA),* became the first Blacks to be elected to Congress from the South, in 74 years.

- *The first National Black Convention* was held in Gary, IN, to advocate for black communities.
- *Shirley Chisholm,* announced her intention to run for President; of the US, a first.
- *Leonard Brown, and Denver Smith* were shot by officers on the campus of *Southern University (LA., an HBCU);* they were among the ongoing protests for "the lack of decent housing conditions, and student funding.
- *"MOVE",* was founded in *Philadelphia, PA, by Vincent Leaphart.* A great controversy over this group followed later.
- *The first group of Haitian Boat People,* arrived in *Florida.* They were not given political asylum.

1973 Maynard H. Jackson of Atlanta, GA.; *Thomas Bradley,* of Los Angeles, CA.; *and Coleman Young* of Detroit, MI., were respectively elected as Mayors.

- ***The Rockefeller Drug Laws,* allowed *indeterminate sentencing, (15 years to life)* for the sale and possession of drugs. *Note: This legislation to crack down on the drug culture of times, created an injustice nightmare that was not corrected until the Obama administration's Fair Sentencing Act.*
- *The Ghetto Information Program,* which *funded informants* for the FBI, was *ended. (see the docudrama Judas and the Black Messiah, 2021).*
- *John Wesley Blassingame became a professor at Yale University, in Afro-American Studies.*

1974 Milliken v. Bradley, the US Supreme Court ruled that school busing was not mandatory, altering its decision of 1971, regarding instances where discrimination was not intentional. ***Note:*** *this ruling encouraged the exodus, or* <u>*white flight*</u> *to the suburbs.*

- ***Morgan v. Hennigan,*** in 1965 *Massachusetts* enacted the **Racial Imbalance Act,** *after the Kerner Report (a government study).* The city of *Boston* refused any attempts to d*esegregate its schools.* A lawsuit was brought by *Morgan, w*ith the help of the *NAACP.* After 9 years. District Court Judge Garrity, ordered busing to achieve it, and <u>oversaw the</u> <u>busing program until 1983.</u>
- *The Auto-Biography of Miss Jane Pittman,* authored by *Edward Gaines,* was published. It depicted the life of African Americans during the Civil War.
- *Black History Month* was established. It went from one week to a month of celebration. The Month of *February* was chosen to honor the birth month of *W.E.B. Du Bois, and Abraham Lincoln.*
- *Barbara Jordan, the Congresswoman from Texas,* gave the opening speech to the Judiciary Committee to Impeach President Nixon (concerning Watergate*). **Note:** The next day, on July 25th, Nixon resigned his Presidency.*
  - ****The Fairness in Lending Act,** *or Equal Credit Opportunity Act (ECOA) of 1974.* along with the **Fair Housing Act***,* attempted to change the banking *lending discrimination* or <u>Redling</u>, which denied financial *opportunities for credit, and homeowner lending. (see the docu-drama The Bankers, 2020)*

1975 There were a lot of first in this year: the first black
TV station owner – William Banks; the first black winner,
of the *Men's Singles at Wimbledon – Arthur Ashe;* the first
black *Airforce 4 Star General - Daniel Chappe James;* the
first black *Major League: Baseball Manager – Frank
Robinson;* the first black participant in golfing's *Master
Tournament – Lee Elders;* the first black *Dean of Medicine
at Morehouse (an HBCU) –* the first black president; of
the *Organization of American Historians – John H
Franklin.*

1976 Barbara Jordan, gave the keynote address at the
Democratic National Convention

- **The Racial Relations Bill of 1976** – *addressed
  any form of decimation against any group of people,
  to provide equal protection under the law.*

*1977 ROOTS, The Saga of an American Family, by Alex
Hailey,* began an 8-day TV mini-series on January 23rd. It
explored unknown history at the time, and a generational
view of one African American family. *Note it was
phenomenal, and gave insights to the slavery existence.*

- *Andrew Young,* formerly of SCLC. and former
  Mayor of Atlanta, GA, was appointed as *US
  Ambassador to the United Nations, by Pres. Carter;
  Patricia Harris,* was appointed as head of *HUD,
  and became the first black woman in a Cabinet
  position.*
- *The Combahee River Collective (CRC) Statement,*
  was made concerning racial and gender oppression
  of black women.

*1978 **Regents of California v. Bakke**, in this case, the US Supreme Court ruled *not to* support racial quotas, but rather to *approve affirmative action.*

- *Minister Farrakhan* re-joined the *Nation Of Islam (NOI),* and distanced himself from the World Community of al Islam.
- *Muhammed Ali,* became the first *3-time* Heavyweight Boxing Champion
- *Faye Wattleton,* became the first black female head of *Planned Parenthood; Jill Brown,* became the first black female *Commercial Pilot.*
- *John Africa, and the MOVE 9,* were convicted, after a shoot-out at *Powelton Village in Philadelphia, PA.;* causing the death of a white police officer, and 18 injuries *(also see the coming entry for 1985, concerning MOVE).*

1979 Hazel Johnson, became the first black female *General, in the US Army.*

- *Assata Shakur, of the Black Panther Party, and their Black Liberation Army,* was serving a life sentence in prison. She escaped in 1979, was added to the FBI 10 most wanted list, but never captured.
- *The Nobel Prize for <u>Economics,</u> went to Sir Thomas Lewis, of Princeton University.*
- ***Brown v. Texas,** in this State Supreme Court ruled on a matter of **4th Amendment** violations in question. The Texas SC ruled that Brown's arrest for not identifying himself, was not valid,* because there was <u>*no probable cause* </u>before the arrest. **Note:** *the state's requirement of identification did*

108

not apply, since there was no other reason to detain Brown. **Also:** *in the future, you will see that the USSC will eliminate the need for" <u>probable cause</u>".*

- **United Steelworkers of America v. Weber,** the US Supreme Court ruled that the **Civil Rights Act of 1974,** did not prevent employers from having affirmative action programs for women, and children. **Note:** *Weber claimed that affirmative action was <u>reverse discrimination towards whites</u>.*

1980 The Miami Liberty Race Riots, occurred between May 17th–20th, due to the court *acquittal* of four Dade County police officers, *who were on trial for manslaughter,* concerning the death of *Arthur McDuffie.* In this instance, after a traffic stop; and a motorcycle chase, Mc Duffie, (a former Marine) died from his *beating injuries,* in 1979.

- *Willie Lewis Brown Jr,* was the first black *Speaker of the House,* for *California.*
- *Toni C Bombara, of Atlanta, GA.,* won the *American Book Award,* for her collection of short stories; *The Salt Eaters.*
- *BET, or Black Entertainment Television, by Robert L Johnson, started network operations in Wash., DC.*

1981 Mumia Abu Jamal, (nee Wesley Cook), a black radio journalist, was accused of the murder of a white police officer, Daniel Faulkner, (on Dec 9th). At that time, he was under surveillance from the FBI, due to his sympathies towards the Black Panthers. He was sentenced to life imprisonment. Through many appeals, his plight gained international attention and support. **Note:** *the activities of*

*COINTELPRO were unknown in those times. **Also**, he remains incarcerated, (as though a political prisoner - see 1971).*

1982 Micheal Jackson, released his iconic album *Thriller*, *in* November, and the rest is history.

- *Bryant Gumbel*, became the first black *anchor* of a major TV network news channel.
- *Environmental Racism* became a national campaign, with the involvement of *Rev. Ben Chavis, a*s he fought against a black neighborhood *toxic waste dump*, in *South Carolina*.
  Note: *this was only one of various ways to eliminate or destroy thriving black communities.*
- *The Color Purple,* a novel written by *Alice Walker, won the Pulitzer Prize for fiction.*
- *A Soldier's Play, by Charles Fuller*, told of the *phenomenon of "Colorism"* among the soldiers of an all-black Army unit. This murder mystery became a movie in 1984; the Soldier's Story. ***Note:*** *also see the entries for the Willie Lynch letter, and the Million Men's March, concerning* <u>*Colorism.*</u>

1983 Vanessa Williams, was crowned as the first black *Miss America. Her title was later vacated.*

- *Guion S Bluford Jr,* became the first black *Aerospace Engineer / Astronaut, in space.*
- *Martin Luther King Jr's* birthday became a *federal holiday.*

- *Robert C Maynard,* took over as owner, publisher, and editor of the *Chicago Tribune,* eventually making it a *Pulitzer Prize winner in Journalism.*
- **Bob Jones University v. The United States,** *the US Supreme Court revoked their tax-exempt status as a religious institution, since they would not admit black students (in prevention of interracial interaction).* **Note:** *Finally, in the year 2000, they admitted blacks.*
- *Harold Washington,* became the first black *Mayor of Chicago.*

1984 W. Wilson Goode, became the first black *Mayor of Philadelphia.*

- ***The Corrections Corporation of America,* was established whereby correctional facilities (jails) *became privately owned (*instead of by the government). **Note:** *as a result, mass incarcerations became a profitable venture (much like slavery) as new drug laws created a huge increase in black imprisonment.*
- *Jesse Jackson,* lost his bid to become the *Democratic nominee for President.*
- *Carl Lewis, matched Jesse Owens' Olympic* gold medal record, for racing.
- *The Bill Cosby Show, made its debut, and became the most successful black family sitcom, for its positive portrayal of a black family, at the time.*
- *Russell Simmons, and Rick Rubin, co-found the hip-hop label, Def Jam Records.*

1985 On May 13ᵗʰ, a confrontation between MOVE, and the Philadelphia police, ended violently with the eventual bombing of their "compound", which was established in a residential neighborhood of the city. Any attempts at negotiation, failed. Five adults, and six children died. A city block of <u>60 homes</u> were razed with the bombing; leaving 250 misplaced (see John Africa, 1978).

- *The Oprah Winfrey Show, became TV legend, and remained for 25 years. Oprah started the OWN network in 2011; which became nationally syndicated. She was also known for her philanthropy.*

*1986 **The Anti-Drug Abuse Act of 1986,** was passed to allow federally mandated sentencing of 5 years, for the sale or possession of crack-cocaine. **Note:** as part of Pres. Reagan's War on Drugs, this created a disproportionate black population increase in prisons (90% by 1990). It took until 2010 for this Act to be corrected by the **Fair Sentencing Act. Also:** This created great profit to the prison system, which became privately owned in 1984.*

- ***Batson v. Kentucky*** ruling by the USSC concerned prosecutors during jury selection. It was ruled that they may not exclude possible jurors based on their race.
- *Spike Lee,* a black filmmaker, released his first movie, *A Woman's Gotta Have It.* He continued to energize the black film industry, winning many awards and an Oscar, for telling *it like it is* and *was.*

- *Mike Tyson, became the youngest boxer to hold the heavyweight title, at age 20.*
- *January 15th, the birthdate of Martin Luther King Jr. was designated a National Holiday. (now celebrated on the third Monday of January).*

*1987 **The Civil Rights Rehabilitation Act,** amended Title IX (which involved financial support for educational facilities; and required compliance with civil rights). This Act was passed in response, and to, and to clarify the ruling of a USSC case, **Grove City College v. Bell.** Eleven years of litigation and laws were clarified, leaving no doubt that education facilities and their attendants must be integrated, on all levels, if they receive federal funds.*

- *Dr. Clifton R. Wharton Jr., became the first black CEO of a Fortune 500 Company, (at TIAA-CREF), which manages pension funds. Later he served as Deputy Secretary of State, under Pres. Clinton. **Note**: not to be confused with the Wharton School of Business, at Univ. of Penn.*
- *The Eyes on the Prize, a two-part documentary by John Louis L Gates Jr., aired on PBS. It reviewed the Civil Rights Movement from 1951 - 1967. Many such documentaries by Gates have given an excellent portrayal of our history.*
- *Rita Dove,* won the *Pulitzer Prize* for excellence in poetry from her book *Museum. Later* she became distinguished as *Poet Laureate.*
- *Dr. Benjamin Carson,* headed a team to separate cerebrally *conjoined twins;* which made history. it took 22 hours; and *they lived.* **Note**: *In 2023, he was*

a Republican candidate (but not nominated) for President of the US.

- *Aretha Franklin,* became the first woman inducted into the *Rock & Roll Hall of Fame; Johnette Coleman* became the first African American *President of Spelman College, an HBCU.*
- *Fences,* a play about black fatherhood, won the *Tony Award,* and *the Pulitzer Prize;* written by *August Wilson.*

1988 Bill Cosby, gifted 20 million dollars to *Spelman College (an HBCU for women).*

- *Temple University, of Philadelphia,* offered the first *Afro American studies PhD.*
- *Toni Morrison* (nee Chloe A Wofford), won the *Pulitzer Prize* for her novel *Beloved,* based on the true story of *Margaret Garner,* a recaptured slave.

1989 The Democratic National Committee, elected Ronald (Ron) H Brown, as its first black chairman; later he became the Secretary of Commerce, in 1993.

- *General Colin Powell, became the first black Chairman of the Joint Chiefs of Staff or National Security Adviser, for Pres. George W. Bush.*
- *Frederic Drew Gregory,* became the first black *Commander of Space Shuttle Discovery, STS-33.* He served a long and distinguished career, and also became *Deputy Administrator of NASA in 2001.*

1990 Douglas Wilder was elected *Governor of Virginia; David Dinkins,* as *Mayor of New York,* and *Norm Rice,*

Mayor of Seattle. Bill White, was elected *President of National League Baseball.*

- *The Civil Rights Act of 1990,* was vetoed by George W Bush. It concerned fair employment litigation.
- *The Americans with Disabilities Act, which prohibited discrimination based on disability, was passed.*
- *Carole Ann-Marie Gist, won the Miss USA Pageant; Walter Massey, headed the National Science Foundation; Donna Marie Cheek, was the first black member of the Equestrian Olympic Team.*
- *August Wilson, won a Pulitzer Prize for his play, The Piano Lesson.*
- *1991 The Rodney King Video* gained national attention when four white policemen were recorded, as they beat a black suspect, after a police chase. *The video was sent to a local news station in Los Angeles;* and viewed by thousands, in 1991.
- *Clarence Thomas,* was seated, as a Justice of the US Supreme Court.
- **The Civil Rights Act of 1991,** amended **Title VII (7), of the Civil Acts Right of 1964,** which addressed the right of employees to sue employers for *discrimination in hiring and promotions.*
- *Henry Louis Gates Jr,* joined the faculty of *Harvard University.* Later, as *Director for the Hutchins Center for African American Research, Prof. Gates launched a prolific* career in documentaries, books, and genealogy, which is current, and unmatched.

1992 The Los Angeles Riots, and protests, involved approx. 7,000 fires; with 63 killed; and 2,373 injured. On

April 29th of 1992, When the policemen involved with the beating of *Rodney King* were *exonerated*, rioting broke out over the following 6 days, *affecting many neighborhoods, cultures, and causing millions in damages.*

- *Mae Jemison,* became the first *African American woman in space, aboard the Endeavor Shuttle.*
- *Spike Lee,* as movie director, released a film on *the life of Malcolm X.*
- *The World Trade Center of NYC was bombed, on February 26th.* **Note:** *this was the first bombing attempt, and should not be confused with the 9/11 disaster of 2001.*

1993 Hazel Reid O'Leary, was appointed as *US Secretary of Energy, by Pres. Clinton.*

- *Carol Mosely Braun,* became the first black female *Democratic Senator of Illinois.*
- *Jocelyn M Elders,* was appointed as *US Surgeon General.*
- *Toni Morrison,* who won the *Pulitzer Prize* for her novel *Beloved, in 1988,* won the *Nobel Prize for Literature*, for that same work, in October.
- *William Pinkney,* became one of *four Americans,* to navigate a *sailboat around the world.*

1994 Dr. Cornel West, of Harvard Univ. published *Race Matters*, which examined the social, political, psychological, and spiritual state of black people, in relation to *"nihilism" (life is meaningless).*

- *O.J. Simpson,* a former football great, *was arrested, for suspicion of the murder* of his wife Nocole Brown, and her friend Ronald Goldman, after an extended police chase, in June.
- *The Willie Lynch Letter, became known around this time, when it was posted on the internet by a college librarian.* It claimed to be a speech from 1712, given on the banks of the *James River, in Virginia.* A pamphlet, called *How to Make a Slave,* based on the letter, is said to have been circulated during the *Million Man March of 1995. Extensive research by myself, by Prof. Manu Ampim,* and others, have revealed that the letter was a fraud. However, the psychological manipulation it revealed was telling *["Keep the Body, Take the Mind"].* **Note:** *"Colorism" (or value by skin tone) among blacks, (and whites towards us), created a breach to keep black people divided. The" slave mentality" was the psychological result of what the letter described. It is only recently that this division has lessened. The "letter" caused blacks to question their racial divide.*
- *Corey Flournoy,* was elected *President of the Future Farmers of America,* and gave the keynote speech for unity, at their Convention in 1995.

*1995 **Miller v. Johnson,** t*he US Supreme Court ruled that states cannot create voting districts based on race, and that *Gerrymandering* was unconstitutional. **Note:** *this decision has currently been weakened by conservative decisions, based on* political affiliation, *instead of race.*

- *The Million Man March* occurred on October 16th. As a day of affirmation, solidarity and support. It showed a positive image of black men. Held on the Washington Mall, it was organized by Minister Louis Farrakhan (Nation of Islam), along with James Bevel, and Benjamin F Chavis Jr (NAACP).

- *Ron Kirk,* became the first black *Mayor of Dallas, Texas.*
- *Dr. Lonnie Bristow,* became the first *African American President of the AMA or American Medical Association.* **Note:** *in previous times. Blacks were not admitted to the AMA.*
- *Helene D, Gayle,* became a *CDC Director of HIV, STD, and TB.*

1996 O.J. Simpson was acquitted of murder, in October. **Note:** *belief in his guilt or innocence was definitely divided along racial lines. The televised trial; dream team of lawyers; and divisiveness between police and blacks, brought fury, and relief, to the respective communities.*

- **Whren v. United States,** the phenomena of *DWB (Driving While Black),* had its day in court. Unfortunately, the case presented by *Whren,* lost. The USSC ruled that being *stopped by police on a mere <u>pretext</u> of wrongdoing was allowable.* Thereby, establishing that a reason for a police stop was no longer necessary. **Note:** *this is the second USSC ruling (see 1968) that absolved police of accountability, concerning shooting blacks. Reasonable cause or suspicion (4th Amendment) were no longer necessary.* **Also:** *The word <u>pretext</u> means, <u>the reason given, is not the real reason.</u> This was a unanimous decision, headed by Justice Scalia.*

- *The Personal Responsibility and Work Opportunity Reconciliation Act (PRWORA),* was passed, sponsored *by Pres. Clinton, in August. This Act* reformed the <u>Welfare System</u> by requiring that recipients work. It also established a limit on Welfare assistance. **Note:** *This was done to decrease generational dependence on the system.*
- *The Illegal Immigration Responsibility Act of 1996 (IIRA),* brough Federal jurisdiction over *immigration, and disenfranchised the amnesty of 1986.* It enforced penalties for those who entered the US within 180–365 days. There was NO means allowed to redress charges, in the reversal of citizenship status.
- *Four Little Girls,* a movie released by director *Spike Lee, documented the death and bombing* event at the 16th St Baptist Church., in 1993 *(which was a retaliation for the Children's Crusade).*
- *California,* voters outlawed *Affirmative Action,* with the passing of *Proposition # 209,* concerning state public organizations, facilities, and businesses.
- *Margaret Dixon,* was elected as the first black President of *AARP.*

1997 The Million Women's March, occurred in Philadelphia, Pa., in October. Organized by Phile Chionesu, and Asia Coney. It encouraged black women, their families, and community. It was attended by 500 575 thousand participants.

- *Harvey Johnson Jr.,* was elected the first black *Mayor of Jackson, MS.;* Patric *Brown,* became

Mayor in Houston, TX.; Lois Jean White, became President of the National Parent Teachers Association.

- *Tiger Woods,* won golfing's *Master's Tournament,* in Augusta, GA.
- *Wynton Marsalis,* was the first jazz [trumpet] composer to win a *Pulitzer Prize.*
- *President Clinton* issued a formal <u>apology</u> speech at the White House, concerning the *Tuskegee Syphilis Study,* which administered the disease to black men, without disclosure. ***Note: The National Research Act was*** *passed to prevent human exploitation, as a result.* ***Personal Note:*** *my own grandfather Curtis, was one of those victims. He was a Minister, and became mentally unstable as a result. At the time, it was shameful to our family.*

1998 James Byrd Jr. was murdered, when three white extremists <u>chained and dragged</u> him for three miles along the back roads of Jasper, TX. ***Note:*** *basketball's Dennis Rodman, donated the funeral expenses for him; the* ***James Byrd Jr. Hate Crimes Prevention Act*** *was passed on 2009; one of the participants was executed in 2019.*

- *John H. Franklin, a* historian, was appointed by Pres. Clinton, to the *Commission on Race,* regarding issues and relations of African Americans.
- *Benjamin Oliver Davis Jr,* became a *4 Star General of the US Air Force.* As a cadet at West Point Academy in 1936, he was ostracized. He was the lead trainer of the *Tuskegee Airmen.* He gave

distinguished service in *WWII,* and was an *activist for the treatment of black soldiers.*

- *Carolyn Jefferson-Jenkins,* was elected President of the *National League of Women Voters.*

1999 *Amadou Diallo* was shot 41 times, by 4 police, for unknown reasons, at his apartment.

- *Maurice Ashley*, became the first black *Chess Grandmaster. Serena Williams.* won the *US Open Women's Singles* tennis match (Althea Gibson was first in 1958). Basketball's *Micheal Jordan,* retired after *six NBA championships.*

INTRODUCTION TO THE 2000'S

At last, we get to the 21st Century. It seems less like history, and more like current events. So far it has been a time of upheaval:

Y2K – 911 – Barack Obama's Presidency – Hurricane Katrina – ICE – Dept of Homeland Security – The first Black President - Obama Care – Shelby v. Holder ruling reversing Civil Rights Act of 1965 – the Black Lives Matter Movement (police killings) – the Charleston, SC killing of 9 church members – 4 blood moons (and upheaval they represented) – The Fair Sentencing Act – Hate Crimes Act; – The international George Floyd Marches, the Pandemic, – Gerrymandering – and Presidential criminal trials – voting controversies - judicial controversies - and the possible dissolution of Democracy as we know it.

2000's

2000 **Gore v. Bush** – the US Supreme Court *determined* the outcome of the Presidential Election in favor of George W Bush. In the state of Florida, the election results were too close to call. An order to recount had to be withdrawn because of time limitations. The *Electoral College votes were given to Bush.* **Note:** *the controversy over electoral college votes and possible manipulation, has become even more important in this century.*

2001 Buildings 1, 2 & 7 of the World Trade Center were *destroyed* in what is now called "9/11". The Twin Towers skyscrapers collapsed from structural damage when 2 airplanes collided into each one of them, causing the death of 2, 977 persons. **Note:** *what is rarely discussed is the structural collapse of building 7, which also housed the headquarters of the FBI and Banking industry (two entities notorious against Blacks), with much history lost. The documentary needed to verify this, is no longer available. More hidden history.*

- *Colin Powell* was appointed *Secretary of State* under *George W Bush.*
- *Condoleezza Rice* became the *National Security Advisor* for *Pres. G W Bush.*

2002 **The Department of Homeland Security Act;** some of the jurisdictions of this Act included emergency *preparedness response, recovery from terrorism responses, public health related activities, bio technology,* whistleblower protection, managing information technology across agencies, federal workforce improvement etc. etc. *BUT it is most noted for the infamous creation of The Department of Immigration and Customs (ICE) in 2003. **Note:** the provisions under this Act could have deterred the Pandemic of 2019, as it did for the Ebola outbreak.*

2003 **Grutter v. Bollinger** the US Supreme Court ruled that *Affirmative Action*, when it is *part of many considerations,_were_permissible.* In this case, a white Law School student's application was denied by the *University of Michigan.*

- *The US Department of Immigration and Customs Enforcement (ICE)* was created in March. It became a feared entity concerning the *deportation of Hispanics. It gave federal jurisdiction authority over state powers.*

2005 Edgar Ray Killen was convicted of the murders of civil rights activists *Goodman, Schwerner, and Cheney.* (See Freedom Summer 1964)

- *Rosa Parks* the Civil rights activist died on Oct 25th; she was *laid-in-state* at the Capitol Hill Rotunda.
- *The Millions More Movement;* a 3-day event on the *Washington Mall* was intended to promote cohesion, interaction, and support; for both men and women; commemorating the *10th anniversary of the Million Man March.*
- *Coretta Scott King,* the wife of MLK Jr. died on January 30th. She was also an activist, and made sure that her husband's legacy didn't die with him.

- *Condoleezza Rice* became the first black female *Secretary of State.*
- *Hurricane Katrina* hit the Gulf Coast, on August 30th, causing an estimated 1,700 lives, many of them African American.

2006 Rep. Cynthia McKinney, who was a 3 term Democrat for Georgia, was remembered for two things:

a. The *Capitol Hill Police* would not acknowledge her identification (DWB), which led to an incident;

b. She gave a *speech introducing impeachment causes* for President Bush regarding the *War with Iraq,* approval to *wiretapping for average citizens,* and *failure to act concerning Hurricane Katrina* (among others). No action was taken because it was at the end of the Congressional session.

- *Spike Lee,* released an HBO documentary, *When the Levees Broke.* It concluded *there was Government failure* on many levels regarding the Levees in New Orleans, and failure to send aid for the mostly black residents of the 4th Ward, after Hurricane Katrina.

2007 Alabama State Trooper James Fowler, was convicted of the murder, in the death of *Jimmie Lee Smith (See 1965);* on May 10th, (42 years after the fact).

- ***Parents Involved in Community Schools v. Seattle School Dist. #1*** – the US Supreme Court did ***not support*** the assignment of students to

School Districts, in order to achieve integration balance.

Barack Hussein Obama II, was elected as the 44th President *of the United States. In his first term we saw the end of Osama bin Laden, Muammar al Qaddafi, and Saddam Hussein, and their reins of terrorism.*

2008 Congress issued an apology for *Slavery and Jim Crow,* to Afro-Americans

- *David A Paterson* became Governor of NY, after the former governor's resignation. He is the 1st governor to be considered legally blind.

2009 Michael Steele Chaired the Republican National Committee, until 2011 when he withdrew. Previously he served as Lt. Gov of MD in 2003-9. Currently (2024) he is a regular commentator for (liberal) MSNBC News (representing a change in political alignment).

The Matthew Shepard and James Byrd Jr. Hate Crimes Prevention Act passed, mandating federal prosecution of all *racially motivated crimes.* (See Byrd 1998)

- *Oscar Grant III* was killed at the Fruitvale Police Station. on Jan. 1, 2009. (see the docu-drama Fruitville Station, 2013).
- *Bernard Monroe* died when he ran from police at a backyard BBQ on Feb. 2, 2009.

2010 ***US Supreme Court v. Kimbrough v Judges*** – on December 10th, a long-awaited correction was made (*re:*

mandatory federal sentencing for possession of crack cocaine versus powder cocaine). This ruling gave Judges permission to *deviate* from the mandated Federal sentencing guidelines of 5 years (to possible lesser).

- ***The Patient Protection and Affordable Care Act*** – also nicknamed *Obama Care*" was passed in March. It was designed to bring sweeping changes and to reform health care circumstances for those who were previously uninsurable, and to protect unwanted disclosure of their personal health information. This has become a *serious political hot button* for left wing politics. ***Note:*** *among the many right-wing oppositions to this Act, are the shared cost responsibility of states to support it, and the expansion of Medicaid, which some states were/are against.*
- ****The Fair Sentencing Act** – allowed *retroactive* consideration and <u>correction </u>for the ***Anti-Drug Abuse Act of 1986***.
- *Kamala Harris, an Afro-Indian female, becomes Attorney General of California.*
- *Alyan Jones* was killed during a raid on 5/16/2010.

2011 Pres. Barack Obama received the *Nobel Peace Prize.*

- *The US Postal Service* issued commemorative stamps to honor 6 Civil Rights leaders
- *Kenneth Chamberlain* was killed when his medical alert triggered on 11/19/2011.
- *The Department of Interior Agriculture* legislated *to repay* Indians and Farmers for past injustices.

2011 *The Martin Luther King Jr.'s* <u>Stone of Hope</u> *statue* was opened on August 22nd, on the National Mall, to commemorate the legacy of his works.

- *Simone Biles* [Owen] a Gymnast of *epic* proportions began a career that continues to the present (2024), as a State, National and International Champion and Olympian.

2012 *Ramarly Graham* was chased into a public bathroom, and shot by police on Feb 12, 2012.

2013 *President Obama* began his 2nd term of office until 2015.

- *Assata Shakur,* who fled the US, was listed on the FBI's 10 *Most Wanted Terrorists.*
- ***Florida v. George Zimmerman,*** who shot *Trayvon Martin* in 2012, while on a <u>neighborhood</u> <u>watch</u> was acquitted of 2nd Degree Murder, in July.
- ****Shelby County (AL) v. Holder*** – the *US Supreme Court* essentially *reversed* the requirements of the **Voter Rights Act of 1965.** *Section 4,* gave oversight to States that had a history of Black voter suppression. Formerly, it provided a *method to monitor accustomed* <u>suppression practices</u>. By declaring *Section 4* <u>unconstitutional,</u> the effect of the 1965 V.R.A was significantly gutted. ***Note:*** *for at least two reasons:* 1. It set the stage for suppression in *all 2016 elections.* 2. It significantly affected a close Governor's race in Georgia (*previously guilty of gerrymandering in 1995*), and possibly other states.

- *Black Lives Matter* became a grassroots *Movement,* established by *Alicia Garza, Opal Tometi, and Patrisse Cullors,* in protest, after the highly publicized incident causing the death *of Trayvon Martin.* **Note:** *the shooting death of Black individuals comes to light occasionally. A true count of actual shootings (approximately 1,000 each year) is available on the website of the Washington Post News.*

2014 The Michael Brown and *Eric Garner* police killings occurred.

- *President Obama* addressed The Global Health Security Summit concerning the outbreak of the *Ebola Virus* in West Africa. He pledged help; requested other countries to do likewise; and instituted measures to prevent its spread in the US. **Note:** *this Presidential action clearly indicates the authority that a President can manage, and was clearly missing during the Pandemic of 2020-21.*
- **Schuette v. Coalition to Defend Affirmative Action** was a case mainly involving university admissions, the DA of the state of Michigan, and any bias. The USSC deferred not to interject between the *state* and *voter* policies or preferences.

2015 At *Emanuel AME Church of Charleston, SC.,* on June 17th, nine (9) people were shot at prayer service by white supremacist *Dylann Roof.* He was sentenced to death for a *Federal Hate Crime.*

- *Loretta Lynch* became the first Afro American female *US Attorney General.*

2016 Donald Trump was elected *President;* and a new cycle of right-wing repression began. ***Note:*** *see an article by* <u>*Candace McDuffie from 1970 - present.*</u>

- *The Smithsonian African American History Museum* opened on the *Mall of Washington, DC* on June 24th. Pres. G W Bush was influential in making this possible.
- *Colin Kaepernick, an NFL Quarterback and activist,* took-a-knee, during the National Anthem (*in protest against police brutality*) It drew national attention and commentary, and ended his football career.

2017 Amanda Gorman became the National Youth *Poet Laureate.*

2018 Ilhan Omar became the first *Islamic Congresswoman* for the state of Minnesota.

THE COVID 19 or *Coronavirus* PANDEMIC officially began on January 20, 2020, and lasted approximately 2 years. *More than 3.7 million deaths occurred, causing economic suppressions and stay-at-home lockdowns in many countries. It was acknowledged by the US in February. Through confusion and mis-information, it was not taken seriously, and caused the death of more than 76,000 in the US, of the many who had the disease.*

2020 Goerge Floyd was murdered in Minneapolis, MN, by police officer *Derek Chauvin*, as he demonstrated *how to subdue a suspect,* to rookie officers (they did not intervene as he died). ***Note:*** *Chauvin was convicted of murder. Solidarity protest marches were held, in the US, and in 60 other countries.* ***Also*** *Policing legislation in this regard has not happened, yet.* The George Floyd Justice in Policing Act *was proposed. It passed by the House of Representatives, but not the Senate.*

- *Koby Bryant,* a basketball legend, and his daughter died in a helicopter crash.

- *Breonna Taylor, and Ahmaud Arbury,* lost their lives as a result of police actions and were added to the *Washington Post* list. ***Note:*** "Say their names" *became a protest chant around this time.*
- *Father Wilton Daniel Gregory* became a Cardinal in the Catholic faith.

2021 Rev. Raphael Warnock became the first Black Senator from Georgia, in a Special Election (he also won his seat again in the *regular* election).

2021 Kamala Harris became the first female *Vice-President,* and secured a majority in the Senate.

••

This is my chance to say that this book cannot possibly include all the events that are part of the black experience; stories and events that others know, and share. Even so, we have given some clarity, and cohesion to our experience; more than was there before. For that opportunity, I thank you.

You may wonder at the amount of American history that is included. It was done to give perspective to our experience. America's history is Black history too. We are the backbone and the back-story of the country. A fuller truth can change perceptions.

Hosea 4:6 KJV My people are destroyed for lack of knowledge...

I'm doing my part.

With Kindest Regards,

CW Porter

Bi-us@constancewporter.com

WHAT NOW BLACK AMERICA?

Each day I listen to the litany of interviews and opinions on our current affairs. It feels like we are just trying to discuss the problem of racial disparity away.

People hope that by virtue of bringing truths to light, it will make a change, but it hasn't. We still have:

- *Criminal actions by people in high places*
- *Unjust Judges*
- *A stagnant Congress, causing much needed changes to be ignored*
- *State and Local laws in direct defiance of the US Constitution*
- *Outright racisms in what were formerly slave states*
- *Backlash on the Civil Rights gains from the last 60 years*

What I know:

From our history, and my research, I realized that my people have tried just about everything. The problem is that, too few know about those efforts; or why they did, or didn't work. You've heard the saying "different ways for different days". That is what we need now.

For example: the (worldwide) marches for George Floyd in Washington on 8/28/20 versus, the original March on Washington on 5/28/63. Both marches were about civil protests, but had different results. THEN vs NOW makes all the difference.

Which brings me back to what now?

THEN: Sixty years ago, we had a leader – who convinced most civil rights organizations to cooperate together for a purpose and a cause; today we don't. Sixty years ago, we had a President who incorporated our cause into his policies. Sixty years ago, we had a congress that wasn't deadlocked.

NOW: Activism – may require a different approach: Find ways to be personally effective, carrying a SIGN is just a start. Immersion - involvement in ANY systems that affect us, especially state and local. Support - find something that works for your interests, or in your area, and support it (like voting for candidates in local elections, or supporting candidates in other important elections.

During the Revolutionary War, it was said that 1/3 of the population were for Freedom, 1/3 were Loyalist to the British, and 1/3 didn't care. Politically, history is repeating itself. Complacency or comfortable indifference is a luxury our people cannot afford. So, jump in and do some splashing around, or be a lifeguard.

REFERENCES

When possible, I have included the source of particular information within the description for that listing. It would be impossible to list the actual websites of most entries.

Here are some of the sites often referenced:

Black Past; African American History, JSTOR, Thought Co, Wikipedia, The Washington Post, The New York Times, Oyez, The US Supreme Court/, Google, Books, Movies; Documentaries; searches for individuals and events; States websites, and US History websites...to name a few. In most cases, sources were cross referenced for additional details, and summarized to the best of my ability.

INDEX

Antao Concalvez	1441
Anthony Johnson	1655
Anthony Burns	1854
Alaine Leroy Locke	1907
A. Philip Randolph	1925 - 36
Adam Clayton Powell Jr.	1945
Alice Coleman	1948
Autherine Lucy Foster	1956
Angela Davis	1970 - 71
Andrew Young	1977
Assata Shakur	1979
Arthur McDuffie	1980
Alice Walker	1982
Aretha Franklin	1987
August Wilson	1987 - 90
Amadou Diallo	1999
Alyan Jones	2010
Assata Shakur	2013
Alicia Garza, Opal Tometi, Patrisse Cullors	2013
Amanda Gorman	2017
Benjamin Banneker	1753
Blanche Kelso Bruce	1875
Booker T. Washington	1895 - 1901
Buchanon v.	1917
Bessie Coleman	1919
Billie Holiday	1939
Bo Jangles Robinson	1939
Benjamin O. Davis Sr. (Genl.)	1940
Benjamin OLliver Davis Jr. (Colonel)	1945 - 54
Bayard Rustin	1947
Boynton v.	1960

Barbara Jordan (Senator)	1972 – 76
Bryant Gumbel	1982
Ben Chavis (Rev.)	1982
Bill Cosby	1984 - 88
Benjamin Carson (Dr,)	1987 – 2023
Benjamin Chavis	1995
Barrack Hussein Obama II	2008 -11 – 13
Bobby Seale	1966 - 2007
Christopher Columbus	
Crispus Attucks	1770
Charles Harrison Mason (Bishop)	1894
Cumming v.	1899
Carter G. Woodson	1915 – 26 - 33
Charles R Drew (Dr)	1938
Crystal Bird Fauset	1938
Charles H. Johnson (Dr)	1946
Claudette Colvin	1956
Clifton Wharton (PhD)	1970
Charles Gordon	1970
Clarence Smith, Edward Lewis, Cecil Hollingsworth, Jonathan Blount	1970
Carl Lewis	1984
Clifton R Wharton Jr. (PhD)	1987
Colin Powell (Genl.)	1989
Carol Ann Marie Gist	1990
Clarence Thomas	1991
Carol Mosely Braun	1993
Corey Flournoy	1994 - 95
Cornel West (Prof)	1994 - 2024
Carolyn Jefferson-Jenkins	1998
Condoleezza Rice	2001
Coretta Scott King	2005
Cynthia McKinney (Rep)	2006

Colin Kaepernick	2016
Denmark Vassey	1822
David Walker	1829
David Ruggles	1834
David Peck	1847
Dred Scott	1857
Daniel Hale Williams (Dr)	1891 - 93
Dorie Miller	1941
Daniel (Chappe) James (Gen.)	1973
Douglas Wilder	1990
David A Paterson	2008
Estaban de Dorantes	1526
Elias Neau	1704
Edward Park Duplex	1888
Earl Lloyd, Chuck Cooper, Nathaniel Clifton	1950
Emmett Till	1955
Ella Baker (SNCC)	1960
Eddie Conway	1971
Edward Gaines	1973
Edgar Ray Killen	2005
Fannie Lou Hamer	1962
Francisco Menendez de Aviles	1565
Frederick Douglas	1841-48-55-74-77-89
Floyd J. Calvin	1927
Frankie Muse (Attorney)	1954
Fred Hampton & Mark Clarke	1969
Frank Robinson	1973
Faye Wattleton	1978
Frederick Drew Gregory (Col)	2005
Gabriel Prosser	1800
George Washington Carver	1896
George Edmond Haynes	1910
Garrett Morgan	1916
George Gibbs Jr.	1941

Gwendolyn Brooks (Dr.)	1950
Guion Buford Jr.	1983
Grutter v. Bollinger	2003
George Floyd	2020
Henry Louis Gates	Intro – 1951 – 87 - 91
Henry Blair	1834
Henry H Garnet (Rev.)	1843
Harriette Tubman	1848
Hariett Beecher Stowe	1852
Harriette Wilson	1859
Henry O. Flipper	1877
Harriet Giles	1881
Henry Smith	1893
Hatte McDaniels	1940
Henrietta Lack	1951
Harry T Moore & Harriett	1951
Huey Newton	1966
Hazel Johnson (Genl.)	1979
Henry Hampton	1987
Hazel Reid O'Leary	1993
Helene Bristow	1995
Harvey Johnson Jr., Patrice Brown, Lois Jean White,	1997
Isabelle de Olivera	1598
Ida B. Wells	1882
ILhan Omar	2018
Jorge Santayana	Intro
John Hawkins (Admiral)	1562
Juan Rodriquez	1613
John Punch	1640
John Casor	1655
Jupiter Hammond	1760
John Hanson	1780
John Baptist Point de Sable	1780
James Healy	1854

John Mercer Langston	1855
June Crumpler	1864
John Willis Menard	1868
John Lewis Ruffin	1869
Judy W. Reed	1884
James & John Johnson	1900
Jimmy Winkfield	1902
Jesse Binga	1921
Jesse Owens	1936
Jane Bolin (Honorable)	1939
James G. Thompson	1941
John H. Johnson	1945 – 51
Jackie Robinson	1947
John H. Franklin	1947
Jessie Blayton	1949
Jaunita Hill	1950
John Howard Morrow	1959
Julian Bond	1960 – 67 - 98
John Lewis (Rep.)	1961 – 63 -64 – 87 - 2020
James Meredith	1962
James Bevel (Rev.)	1962
Jimmy Lee Smith	1965
James Farmer (Esq.)	1942 – 45 – 46 – 60 - 61
Jesse Jackson (Rev.)	1971 - 84
John Africa	1978 - 85
Jocelyn Elders	1993
James Byrd Jr.	1998
John H Franklin	1998
Jimmie Lee Smith	1965 - 2007
King Ferdinand & Queen Isabella	1492
King Phillip II	Afro existence
King Charles I, King Charles V of Spain, Holy Roman Emperor	1452, 1518
Kamala Harris	2010 - 24

Kenneth Chamberlin	2011
Lucas Vasquez	1526
Loving v.	1967
Leroy "Satchel" Page	1971
Leonard Brown & Denver Smith	1972
Lonnie Bristow	1995
Loretta Lynch (AG)	2015
Mulana Karenga	Intro - 1966
Mathieu de Costa	1603
Mathias de Sousa	1641
Macon Bolling Allen	1845
Mary Eliza Mahoney	1879
Mary McLeod Bethune	1904 – 35 - 36
Madame C. J. Walker	1906
Matthew Henson	1909
Marcus Garvey	1916 - 24
Murrey v.	1935
Morgan. v.	1946
Minnie Jocelyn Elders	1953
Mary Terrell	1953
Malcolm X	1954 - 65
Martin Luther King Jr	1957 - 58 - 60 - 63 - 64 – 65 – 68 - 86
Medgar Evers	1963
Maulana R Karenga	1966
Maynard H Jackson	1973
Minister Farrakhan (NOI)	1978
Mumia Abu Jamal	1981
Michael Jackson	1982
Mike Tyson	1986
Mae Jamison	1992
Miller v.	1995
Margaret Dixon	1996
Maurice Ashley	1999

Michael Steele	2003-7, 2011, 2024
Michael X Garrett Sr. (Genl.)	2019
Nat Turner	1831
Norris Wright Cuney	1886
Norris v.	1935
Nat King Cole	1956
Ossian (Dr) & Henry Sweet	1925 - 26
Oprah Winfrey	1985
O J Simpson	1994
Oscar Grant III	2009
Pedro Alonzo Nina	1492
Ponce de Leon	1513
Pope Nicholas V	1455
Phyllis Wheatley	1773
Paul Cuffe	1780
Prince Hall	1787
Pinkney Benton Stewart (PBS) Pinchback	1872
Patrick Healy (Bishop)	1873
Pace v.	1883
Plessy v.	1895
Paul Robeson	1932 - 46
Pauli Murray (Rev. Dr.)	1940 - 66
Parez v. (re: Sylvester Davis)	1948
Phile Chionesu & Asia Coney	1997
Queen Ann of GB	1711
Richard Allen	1787
Robert Smalls	1865
Ruby Standish Baldwin	1910
Roy Wilkins	1934
Ralph Bunch	1950 - 63
Rosa Parks	1956
Robert L Johnson	1980
Robert C Maynard	1983
Rita Dove	1987

Rodney King	1991 - 92
Ron Kirk	1995
Ramarly Graham	2012
Raphael Warnock (Sen)	2021
Stono / Cato	1739
Sojourner Truth	1851
Strauder v.	1880
Sophia Packard	1881
Samuel Davidson	1885
Solomon Carter Fuller	1904
Solomon Carter Fuller	1921
Smith v.	1944
Shelly v.	1948
Stokely Carmichael	1960 - 66
Shirley Chisholm	1968 - 70
Swann v.	1971
Sir Thomas Lewis	1979
Spike Lee (Dir.)	1986 - 92
Simone Biles	2011 - 24
Thomas Jennings	1820
Theodore Sedgewick	1827
Thomas Mundy Peterson	1870
T. Thomas Fortune	1887
The Scottsboro Boys	1931
Timmie Rogers	1948
Thurgood Marshall (Hon.)	1954 - 67
The Little Rock 9	1957
Tommie Smith & John Carlos	1968
Toussaint L'Ouverture	1790
The Soledad Brothers	1970
Toni Morrison / Margaret Garner	1988 - 93
Tiger Woods	1997
Trayvon Martin	2013
Vernon Jordan (Esq.)	1960

Vincent Leaphart	1972
Vanessa Williams	1983
Winston Churchill	Intro
William Tucker	1624
William Still	1843
William Wells Brown	1853
Willam C Nell	1855
William (Wille) Lee	1863
W.E.B. Du Bois	1895 – 1903-09
Wallace Fard Mohammed	1930
Walter White	1931
William A. Hinton (Prof)	1948
Wesley Brown	1948
William Hinton	1949
Wesley A Brown (Col.)	1949
William Banks	1973
Willie Lewis Brown Jr.	1980
W. Wilson Goode	1983
William Pinkney	1993
Whren v.	1996
Wynton Marsalis	1997
York	1804

www.ingramcontent.com/pod-product-compliance
Lightning Source LLC
Chambersburg PA
CBHW051206120626
46547CB00013B/1226